# 100 Years of Hilltop and Valley-Bottom Cricket:

## The Centenary History of the Halifax Cricket League 1914 - 2014

Written and Compiled by
**Peter Davies**
and
**David Normanton**

Published by Andrew Smith
May 2014

First published in 2014 by:
Andrew Smith
19 Stones Drive, Ripponden, Sowerby Bridge
West Yorkshire HX6 4NY

British Library Cataloguing-in-Publication data:
A catalogue record for this book is available from the British Library.

ISBN 978-0-9565325-1-0

Printed and bound by: **CPL** design+print  348 Station Road, Bamber Bridge, Preston, Lancashire, PR5 6EL

Front cover:

Comparison of Clubhouses
Blackley CC - around 1910
Copley CC - 2014

# Contents

# Forewords

## David Normanton, Current League President

The purpose of this book is to act as a celebration of the 100th anniversary of the Halifax Cricket League and its intention to try to capture a flavour of what has happened in all those years.

The League has been built on the dedication and hard work of past and present officials and by the many committee members that have served on various committees, to run the organisation over those 100 years.

The task of putting together such a document has not been an easy job and has only been achieved by the perseverance of a small number of dedicated individuals combined with the wealth of information available through the Cricket Heritage Project, the commitment and compilation skills of Peter Davies and the substantial input from well known characters and stalwarts from our clubs both past and present.

John Arlott and Fred Trueman are quoted as referring to cricket -"Most games are skin deep but cricket goes to the bone" and Sir Neville Cardus said that "The elements are cricket's presiding geniuses" and "It is far more than a game, this cricket". All very apt sayings to describe in a nutshell what cricket means and has meant to our local communities.

Local cricket is awash with countless anecdotes, stories and characters and our local cricket game achieves a great deal of its impact in the way it reflects the idiosyncrasies and passions of life. So to try to condense 100 years of those items into a publication demands a respectful balance of fairness between availability of information and quality of relevance when deciding what to put in and what to leave out.

This book I believe will take you on a fascinating journey through our local cricket history created by our valley bottom clubs by the rivers and streams, meandering your way past a number of clubs who have created their own cricket haven on the middle ground, taking you to the clubs at the very top of our hills where magnificent scenery provides a perfect backdrop for our equally beautiful game. The people, the places, the clubs and the communities that have combined to form our League over these years can be re-lived in the photographs, facts, figures and stories that are shared with you the reader. I hope you very much enjoy looking at the pictorial evidence and gain much pleasure from reading this publication.

# Barry Tennyson, League Chairman, 1992-2010

My period of office as League Chairman came about due to the sudden death of the then chairman, Alan Sutcliffe, a former member and player with SBCI CC. At that time I was the League Press Officer and was somewhat surprised when the President, Terry Wynne, asked me to take the office of Chairman on a temporary basis until the next AGM when I was formally elected.

During my time as Chairman, I was fortunate to work alongside many dedicated and hardworking officers of our League, namely Terry Wynne, President (Bradshaw CC), followed by the current President, David Normanton (Stones), Secretaries: Leyland Smith (Sowerby Bridge) and Keith Goulden (Copley), Treasurers Harry Schofield (Barkisland), David Normanton (Stones), and Robert Airey (Outlane), and Fixture Secretaries Michael Sheppard and Brian Laycock, both of Sowerby St Peter's.

During this period the Halifax Cricket League has gone from strength to strength both on and off the field and is now recognised as one of the leading amateur leagues in the whole of Yorkshire. Facilities have improved both on and off the field with most clubs now having bars that generate much needed finances for ground improvement, new electronic scoreboards and funds for junior coaching.

On a personal level I was proud to introduce the current T20 competition that has provided much needed income in the early rounds with home fixtures for all clubs and then a most popular Finals Day now held at the end of July.

Also, serving for many years on the Collinson Memorial Committee gave much pleasure to not only myself but also the numerous older cricketers, to enable our young talented cricketers to go to the now defunct Scarborough Cricket Week for intensive coaching, with a number of boys going on to play in higher grade cricket, some as far as county level.

Through involvement with junior cricket I met many like-minded cricket enthusiasts throughout Yorkshire whose aim is to help the young players of our respective leagues.

The highlight of my term of office was being put forward by our president David Normanton for the Yorkshire Cricket Board OSCA's, where I was fortunate to win the Leagues and Boards award for 2011. This enabled me to go to the home of cricket, Lord's, where an unforgettable day was enjoyed, meeting numerous present-day England players.

All in all I have enjoyed 19 years of wonderful memories serving our League and I wish the Halifax Cricket League much success in the next 100 years.

# Introduction

Welcome to the Centenary History of the Halifax Cricket League.

It was a great honour to be asked to research this book and I have thoroughly enjoyed putting it together.

I live in Huddersfield and started getting to know the cricket clubs and grounds of Calderdale in the early 2000s when I wrote a short book about the cricket clubs and grounds of the area, *Home Soil*.

I loved the grounds that I visited and I came to realise what a beautiful place Calderdale was.

Then, as a university lecturer, in 2004 I applied to the Heritage Lottery Fund (HLF) for a grant to research and reconstruct the history of cricket in Calderdale and Kirklees – an area which is now home to around 100 clubs.

I was successful, able to employ a research assistant, and thus set out on an amazing journey – both literal and metaphorical. We had £50,000 to play with and we used the money wisely. We researched club histories, put on exhibitions, arranged discussion meetings, hired an artist, painter and photographer to capture cricketing landscapes, set up an interactive website, staged an evening course, led workshops, wrote classroom sessions for schools, and devised cricketing walks. We had a truly fantastic time.

And we also got to know the Halifax Cricket League very, very well. We travelled up and down the area, interviewing club officials, going to matches and researching the year-by-year history of each club. We also wanted our project to be totally inclusive, so we put a major emphasis on women – as players, spectators, and, of course, tea ladies.

Throughout, we were in constant touch with club officials and League officers, and David Normanton and his colleagues became key contacts.

Like everyone reading this book, I also spend a lot of time watching cricket. Every Saturday, me and my Dad travel round four or five grounds and enjoy ourselves totally, journeying from village to village, enjoying the cut and thrust of local League competition, and obviously, also, relishing our cricket teas.

This book has been a joy to research and write.

Since 2004, the Calderdale and Kirklees Cricket Heritage Project has been a constant in my life and, when I knew that the Halifax Cricket League would be celebrating its centenary in 2014, I was keen to be involved.

My philosophy during the preparation of this book has been simple. I have wanted to portray the Halifax Cricket League in its true light – as a worthy and well organised competition. But more than that, I have sought to bring to life the people, places and clubs that have made the Halifax Cricket League the wonderful institution that it is.

Our project research has obviously been crucial to this. Since 2004 we have located thousands and thousands of local cricketing images and documents, and I hope I have done justice to these by including as many of them as possible in the pages that follow.

So I make no apology for saying that this is very much a pictorial or visual history of the League. What do they say? A picture paints a thousand words? Too true. If ever a history project has gone big on images, it has been our HLF cricket project, and I have wanted to reflect this in this book. To me, the images here are so fundamentally powerful – and I hope you agree.

Thank you to Dr Rob Light, Brian Heywood, and many others for their help with the original research. And to David Normanton, Leyland Smith and Stephen Williams for their help in the preparation of this book.

*Peter Davies*

# Patrons

The Halifax Cricket League would like to thank all the following who have contributed financially towards the publication of this book.

Robert A Airey
Anne J Airey
David J Bates
Stephen M Beverley
J. Keith Beverley
Gary Boocock
Karen Boocock
Anthony Briggs
Peter Butterfield
Roy Chappell
Keith Clay
Andrew Cleveland
John & Carol Cliff & Family
Alan Conyers
Geoff Cowgill
John Dixon
Alan Ford
Mark Gill
Martin Goldsborough
G Eddie Griffiths
Duncan Hall
Peter J Halstead
George Phillip Hamer
Allen Hampshire
Keith Hartley
Mark Hassall
Tim Helliwell
Les Helliwell
Richard Hemblys
Tony Heptinstall
Derrick Hopkinson
Simon Howard
Tony & Rosemary Hoyle
Peter Hoyle
Richard Hoyle

Anthony Hubbert
David J Hudson
Keith Hudson
James Hudson
Martin Jenkins
Ray Jordan
Steve Jordan
Allen Jowett
Ian Jowett
Derek Kitchen
Brian Lawrence
Trevor Laycock
Geoff, Robert, Richard & Anne Laycock
Willie Laycock
Brian Laycock
Brian Lymbery
Andy Mellor
Andrew Mitchell
Neil Myers
Peter & Janet Myers
David J Neal
David Normanton
Matthew Normanton
Edward Owens
Julie Pearson
Mabel Pighills
Richard Pinder
Stephen G Priestley
Brian Pryke
Andrew Rawnsley
Paul Rowbotham
Sophia Rowbotham
Michael Sheppard
Leyland Smith

Howard Smith
Michael A Smith
P. Andrew Smith
Paul Smithies
Ray Speight
John Stanger
Stuart Stokes
John Sunderland
Jonny Sykes
Raymond Taylor
Peter Taylor
John Taylor
Barry Tennyson
Trevor Tetley
Peter Tetley
Stephen Tomlinson
Joseph E Townsend
Rodney Wade
Keith Walker
Simon Walker
Robert N Wilkinson
Stephen Williams
Geoff Wright
Keith Yates

Copley Cricket Club
Greetland Cricket Club
Mytholmroyd Cricket Club
Old Crossleyans Cricket Club
Outlane Cricket Club
Queensbury Cricket Club
SBCI Cricket Club
Stones Cricket Club
Wibsey Park Chapel Cricket Club

PROUD SPONSORS OF THE HALIFAX CRICKET LEAGUE

For more information about our brands , services and support packages

please call Heineken UK on 0845 8787074

Please enjoy our brands responsibly

www.heineken.co.uk

# The League in 2014

## Officers

**President:**
David Normanton
E-mail: president@halifaxcricketleague.co.uk

**Chairman:**
Anthony Briggs
E-mail: chairman@halifaxcricketleague.co.uk

**Hon. Secretary:**
Neil Myers
E-mail: secretary@halifaxcricketleague.co.uk

**Hon. Asst. Secretary (Minutes):**
Alan Ford
E-mail: forda1@sky.com

**Hon. Disciplinary Officer:**
Alan Ford
E-mail: forda1@sky.com

**Hon. Treasurer:**
Bob Airey
E-mail: treasurer@halifaxcricketleague.co.uk

**Hon. Fixture Secretary:**
Peter Taylor
E-mail: fixture@halifaxcricketleague.co.uk

**Hon. Press Secretary:**
Geoff Wright
E-mail: press@halifaxcricketleague.co.uk

**Hon. League Welfare Officer:**
Neil Myers
E-mail: neilmyers2010@hotmail.co.uk

**League Historian:**
Dr. Peter Davies
E-mail: peterdavies80@hotmail.co.uk

# Member Clubs 2014

1. Blackley CC
2. Booth CC
3. Bradshaw CC
4. Bridgeholme CC
5. Clayton CC
6. Copley CC
7. Cullingworth CC
8. Denholme Clough CC
9. Greetland CC
10. Jer Lane CC
11. Low Moor Holy Trinity CC
12. Luddendenfoot CC
13. Mytholmroyd CC
14. Northowram Hedge Top CC
15. Old Crossleyans CC
16. Old Town CC
17. Outlane CC
18. Oxenhope CC
19. Queensbury CC
20. Shelf CC
21. Southowram CC
22. Sowerby Bridge CC
23. SBCI CC
24. Sowerby St. Peter's CC
25. Stainland CC
26. Stones CC
27. Thornton CC
28. Triangle CC
29. Warley CC
30. Wibsey Park Chapel CC

# Member Clubs 1914 - 2014

**In order of first joining the League**

| | | |
|---|---|---|
| 1 | CLIFTON BRITANNIA | 1914 - 1915 AND 1924 - 1936 |
| 2 | GREETLAND | 1914 - |
| 3 | ILLINGWORTH ST MARY'S / ILLINGWORTH(FROM 1950) | 1914 - 1919 AND 1942 |
| 4 | LIGHTCLIFFE | 1914 |
| 5 | NORWOOD GREEN | 1914 - 1940 |
| 6 | SIDDAL | 1914 - 1915, 1922 - 1939 AND 1949 - 1994 |
| 7 | SOWERBY BRIDGE | 1914 - 1915 AND 1985 - |
| 8 | STAINLAND | 1914 - |
| 9 | TRIANGLE | 1914 - |
| 10 | ELLAND EDGE | 1914 - 1916 |
| 11 | MYTHOLMROYD | 1915 - |
| 12 | BOOTH | 1919 - 1920, 1938 - 1942 AND 1947 - |
| 13 | HALIFAX BAPTISTS | 1919 - 1922 |
| 14 | SIDDAL UNITED | 1919 |
| 15 | SOWERBY ST PETER'S | 1920 - 1921 AND 1923 - |
| 16 | ELLAND A | 1921 - 1923 |
| 17 | NORLAND | 1921 |
| 18 | NORTHOWRAM (NOW REFORMED AS NORTHOWRAM FIELDS) | 1921 - 1922 |
| 19 | TURNER & WAINWRIGHTS / TURNWRIGHTS & CLIFTON (FROM 1937) | 1922 - 1936 AND 1937 - 1939 |
| 20 | COPLEY | 1923 - |
| 21 | SMITH BULMERS | 1929 - 1930 |
| 22 | HALIFAX B (INITIALLY 3RD XI THEN 2ND XI) | 1930 - 1934 AND 1940 |
| 23 | HEATH OLD BOYS | 1930 - 1934 |
| 24 | STONES METHODIST'S / STONES (FROM 1971) | 1937 - |
| 25 | BARKISLAND | 1939 - 2000 |
| 26 | BLAKEBOROUGH'S (SPORTS ASSOCIATION) | 1939 - 1942, 1944 - 1946 AND 1951 - 1956 |
| 27 | DEAN CLOUGH / CROSSLEY'S CARPETS (FROM 1963) | 1939 - 1980 |
| 28 | ARMY XI (BASED AT OVENDEN PARK BARRACKS) | 1944 - 1945 |

# League Officials 1913 - 2014

## PRESIDENTS

| | |
|---|---|
| 1913 | J.A. SHUTTLEWORTH |
| 1914 - 1915 | J. E. SHAW |
| 1916 - 1918 | J. E. CLARKSON |
| 1919 - 1928 | J. J. FIELDEN |
| 1929 - 1946 | H. CLARK |
| 1947 - 1964 | H. WHITEHEAD |
| 1965 - 1970 | N. E. CROSSLEY |
| 1971 - 1987 | R. SMITH |
| 1988 - 2003 | T. WYNNE |
| 2004 - | D. NORMANTON |

## SECRETARIES

| | |
|---|---|
| 1913 - 1921 | G. HOLDSWORTH |
| 1922 - 1947 | H. WILSON |
| 1948 - 1964 | N. E. CROSSLEY |
| 1965 - 1988 | S. HIRST |
| 1989 - 2008 | L. SMITH |
| 2009 - 2010 | K. GOULDEN |
| 2011 - | N. MYERS |

## TREASURERS

| | |
|---|---|
| 1914 - 1915 | J. A. CROWTHER |
| 1916 - 1945 | J. H. TAYLOR |
| 1946 - 1947 | N. E. CROSSLEY |
| 1948 - 1963 | S. PARKER |
| 1964 - 1974 | W. LAYCOCK |
| 1975 - 1995 | H. SCHOLEFIELD |
| 1996 - 2003 | D. NORMANTON |
| 2004 - | R. A. AIREY |

## CHAIRMEN

This Office was only introduced as the President Mr Clark suffered ill health.
Mr Teal, a member of the executive at the time, was asked to Chair.
The official position was created and he was duly elected in 1944.

| | |
|---|---|
| 1943 - 1961 | G. TEAL |
| 1962 - 1970 | R. SMITH |
| 1971 - 1977 | R. CHAPPELL |
| 1978 - 1987 | T. WYNNE |
| 1988 - 1991 | A. SUTCLIFFE |
| 1992 - 2010 | B. TENNYSON |
| 2011 - | A. BRIGGS |

**The following officers were introduced as stated:**

## PUBLICITY OFFICER

| | |
|---|---|
| 1935 - 1949 | A. SUNDERLAND |

## FIXTURE SECRETARIES

| | |
|---|---|
| 1961 - 1979 | J. H. STOTT |
| 1980 - 2005 | M. J. SHEPPARD |
| 2006 - 2008 | B. LAYCOCK |
| 2009 - | P. TAYLOR |

## PRESS SECRETARIES

| | |
|---|---|
| 1976 - 1978 | H. WHITELEY |
| 1979 - 1986 | I. H. BALDWIN |
| 1987 - 1993 | B. TENNYSON |
| 1994 - 1995 | D. NORMANTON |
| 1996 - 2001 | G. LAYCOCK & B. LAYCOCK |
| 2002 - 2005 | B. LAYCOCK |
| 2006 - | G. WRIGHT |

## ASSISTANT SECRETARIES

| | |
|---|---|
| 1987 | A. SUTCLIFFE |
| 1988 | L. SMITH |
| 1989 - 1998 | NO APPOINTMENTS |
| 1999 | T. ATKINSON |
| 2000 - 2005 | N. MYERS |
| 2006 | NO APPOINTMENT |
| 2007 - 2008 | K. GOULDEN |
| 2009 | L. SMITH |
| 2010 | A. BRIGGS |
| 2011 - | A. FORD |

## ASSISTANT FIXTURE SECRETARY

| | |
|---|---|
| 2009 - 2012 | B. LAYCOCK |

## CHILD WELFARE OFFICER

| | |
|---|---|
| 2009 - | N. MYERS |

## ASSISTANT SECRETARY REGISTRATIONS

| | |
|---|---|
| 2010 - | N. MYERS |

## ASSISTANT SECRETARY DISCIPLINE

| | |
|---|---|
| 2010 - 2013 | T. HEPTINSTALL |
| 2014 - | A. FORD |

# A Potted History of the League

## THE HALIFAX PARISH CRICKET LEAGUE 1914-1925 AND THEN
## THE HALIFAX CRICKET LEAGUE 1926 ONWARDS
## A POTTED HISTORY OF THE LEAGUE

### WRITTEN AND COMPILED BY DAVID NORMANTON

So, how did the Halifax Cricket League come to life and why?

I have to take you back to 1913.

At that time there were already a number of cricket leagues in Halifax comprising of:-
The Halifax Amateur Cricket League 1892
The Halifax & District Cricket League 1896
The Halifax & District Church Sunday School League 1907
The Halifax & District Non-Conformists League 1908

So two Leagues had been established for 20 years and two for just over 5 years. A lot of cricket was being played.

It is the Halifax & District Cricket League we must turn our attention to. That League had made a decision in 1913 that caused a great deal of discontent amongst the clubs of that League. The decision made was to revert back to the old order of two divisions from the one division currently being operated.

The League had been divided into two divisions in 1908 but in 1912 reverted back to a one division structure of 19 teams, who played 16 matches with a top 4 play-off.

In 1913 the League attempted to attract better class clubs to allow expansion to two large divisions. However, no clubs came forward but the decision was still made to revert back to two divisions with the top 10 clubs in 1913 forming division one.

The clubs with the better class grounds had not been performing well and so occupied the lower positions. This unease about being placed in the 2nd division for 1914, coupled with the concern of the overall standard of pitches, led to a breakaway League being discussed.

On the 29th July 1913 a meeting was convened at the Upper George Hotel, Halifax led by Siddal and they were joined by Sowerby Bridge, Stainland, Greetland, Illingworth, Norwood Green, Triangle, 7 of them, with invites to 3 other clubs – Clifton Britannia, Lightcliffe and Ovenden.

Mr J A Shuttleworth (Stainland) was elected President
Mr J A Crowther (Sowerby Bridge) Treasurer, and
Mr G Holdsworth, Secretary

The irony being, that two of these gentlemen occupied these same two positions in the Halifax & District Cricket League and had done so for a long number of years. Mr Shuttleworth was also a past President of the Parish Cup Committee, so all were very influential local cricket characters.

The decision was taken to form a new League in 1914, the Halifax Parish Cricket League and as you will appreciate it was a move which was quite controversial at that time. The officers and clubs did not want any ill-feeling but stressed the issue was to be viewed as enterprising on the part of the clubs concerned and to have better club cricket. Clubs forming the new League were Siddal, Triangle, Clifton Britannia, Greetland, Lightcliffe, Norwood Green, Sowerby Bridge, Elland Edge, Illingworth St Mary's and Stainland.

In 1914, due to landlord trouble, Ovenden became defunct and Elland Edge accepted their place after an invitation.

The original League comprised 10 clubs and remarkably 6 of these clubs remain in existence today. Triangle, Greetland, Sowerby Bridge and Stainland all play in the Halifax League, whilst

Lightcliffe play in the Bradford League and
Illingworth in the Aire & Wharfe League

Another decision taken then was that professionals would not be allowed. Professionals were allowed in the Halifax & District League. This issue was strongly debated with some clubs wanting more than one professional.

League Meetings would be held on Tuesdays and still are to this day.

Only matches won outright would count as points, draws and losses were ignored.

Two-thirds of matches had to be played for a win to count.

August 15th was the local holiday date and this was left open thus giving clubs no concern and worry raising teams over the 'Wakes' holiday.

All playing members had to reside within a radius of 5 miles of their own club ground or have played 4 successive seasons with that club unless special sanction was obtained from the Management Committee.

These rules were innovative and different at that time to other Leagues in existence.

So on the 25th April 1914 the first matches were played, and on the 19th April 2014 the next season began, commencing the next 100 years of Halifax League cricket.

These founder clubs were all local village sides with only Illingworth showing any belonging to a church. They covered a relatively wide area of the then Halifax Parish, but mirrored the topography of the area with valley bottom clubs at Triangle, Sowerby Bridge and Greetland, but in the main hill top clubs, Clifton Britannia playing on a field behind the Armitage Arms at the top of a hill, Illingworth on the hill tops above Halifax, Stainland on the other side of Halifax high on the hills. The only relatively flat pieces of ground could be found either at the valley bottom or high up on the hills which are a feature of Halifax and the surrounding areas or Calderdale as it is known today.

The first AGM took place on 27th October 1914 at the Upper George, and the second one on the 9th November 1915. AGM's are still to this day held in November, now on the third Tuesday in the month.

With the on-set of World War One at the end of the first season it is incredible that the League survived at all!

In 1915 Lightcliffe left and Mytholmroyd took their place. Sowerby Bridge, Siddal and Clifton Britannia also left to join a Halifax Section of the Yorkshire Council.

Now only seven clubs competed in 1916 and the War was at its worst so the League was suspended in 1917 and 1918 before returning to League action in 1919.

The League remained under the Officership of those two stalwarts at that time, Secretary Holdsworth and Treasurer Taylor. However, the League was now under the Presidency of a Mr J J Fielden who had held the office of Vice President from 1914 to 1918. He was the fourth President in 6 years. The office of Vice President was never brought back for an individual.

In 1919 the League commenced again with 9 clubs:
Greetland, Illingworth, Norwood Green, Stainland, Triangle, (five of the original ten) Mytholmroyd (from 1915) and these were joined by Siddal United, Halifax Baptist's and Booth.

In 1920 the League dropped to 8 clubs, when Illingworth moved to the Yorkshire Council Halifax Section and Sowerby St. Peter's replaced Siddal United.

The War had taken its toll and times were difficult but they managed to survive and pull through even though in 1920 Norland were not accepted due to the most difficult route to get to the ground, yet they were accepted in 1921. Playing for just that one year, when they were back to 10 clubs.

In 1921 Booth left; down to 7 clubs but applications from Elland A, Norland and Northowram (now reformed as Northowram Fields) were accepted making it back to 10 clubs.

In 1922 Siddal rejoined, Norland and Sowerby St. Peter's went back to the Halifax & District League for one year before that League merged to form the Halifax & District Amateur League in 1923 with the final place taken up once again by Clifton Britannia – 10 again.

In 1923 Halifax Baptists left along with Northowram, both never to return, and they were replaced by Sowerby St. Peter's and Copley.

In 1924 the League consisted of Clifton Britannia, Mytholmroyd, Greetland, Norwood Green, Sowerby St. Peter's, Siddal, Triangle, Copley, Stainland and the wonderfully named Turner & Wainwrights, a works side who joined in 1922. The League then remained at these 10 clubs until 1929.

In 1926 the League dropped the word Parish from its title and became known as the Halifax Cricket League, a title it has held to this present day.
In 1929 Smith Bulmers, a textile workers side who had won the Halifax Association League in

1927 and 1928, were accepted making an odd number of 11 clubs. The club only lasted two years and this short span playing in a better standard of cricket actually led to their demise, when they finished bottom in 1930.

In 1930 Halifax B, initially a 3rd XI but from 1932 their 2nd XI, who won the League in 1932 and 1933 and Heath Old Boys were accepted making 13.

In 1931 however, the League was back at 12 clubs with Smith Bulmers demise. The League constituted as follows: Halifax, Siddal, Turner & Wainwrights, Stainland, Greetland, Sowerby St. Peter's, Heath Old Boys, Copley, Clifton Britannia, Mytholmroyd, Norwood Green and Triangle.

Through the 30's the League comprised between 10 and 13 clubs before surprisingly in 1939 the League expanded to 14 clubs with Barkisland, Blakeboroughs and Dean Clough all joining in 1939, (my own club) Stones Methodist's were admitted in 1937 and Booth were back in 1938.

In 1937 Turner & Wainwrights amalgamated with Clifton to form Turnwrights & Clifton from 1937 to 1939, but when War broke out the ground at Brookfoot was ploughed up. The future again looked reasonable but 1939 was to see the outbreak of War.

For a second time the League was to endure a World War lasting two years longer than the first, only this time the League managed somehow to play through each year with only the Second XI competition being suspended from 1941 to 1945. However, it states in the Minutes that although most teams were maintained they failed to do themselves justice!

League Meetings were well attended characterised by good fellowship and mutual respect.

In 1941 Copley and Norwood Green retained membership by paying Vice Presidents subscriptions but in 1942 Norwood Green disbanded.

Two Wartime sides played in the League. An Army XI in 1944 and 1945 from the 105 Military Convalescent Department from the Ovenden Park Camp and in 1945 a second Army side joined for one year: Re-Dep formed out of the men at the HQ of the Royal Engineers Depot who played their matches at Copley.

In 1944 another point of wartime interest was the minutes reported that the League had 15 umpires, 7 of whom were unattached.

At this time (1944) clubs were requesting that the rules needed revision, in particular rules governing cancellation of matches.

Clubs raised money for the Red Cross and St. John's Ambulance during the War effort.

During the period 1937 to 1948 the outstanding club was Mytholmroyd, their achievements in this period will probably never ever be repeated again. Their 1st XI were Champions on no less than 8 occasions and their 2nd XI were Champions on 5 occasions out of 7 played. In 1948 they did the treble because a 3rd XI or Junior Section was introduced and Mytholmroyd made a clean sweep of each Championship. C Pugh and H Wilcock achieved an identical bowling record for the League's 1st XI Bowling Prize both finishing with 71 wickets at a cost of 475 runs giving them both an average of 6.69. No less a figure than the great Sir Len Hutton was invited and duly attended their Presentation Evening.

After the War in 1946 the League commenced with 10 clubs constituted as follows:

Barkisland, Blakeboroughs, Copley, Dean Clough, Greetland, Mytholmroyd, Sowerby, Stainland, Stones Methodists and Triangle. With only 4 of those clubs being able to turn out a Second XI, namely Greetland, Mytholmroyd, Stones and Triangle.

The Executive were strongly criticised for not bringing forward the requested rules revision from 1944.

Having met at the Upper George since its inception the League moved its Meeting HQ to another pub, The Plummet Line in the centre of Halifax, and met there for the first time in April 1946 under a new President, Harold Whitehead of Stones. At that meeting Stainland and Barkisland indicated they could now raise a 2nd XI, so it was agreed to revise all the 2nd XI fixtures for 1946.

The League continued with 8 ball overs.

In 1947 all clubs ran 2nd XI's and the rules revision was approved en bloc at last! The League then expanded rapidly over the next 6 years. In 1947 and 1948 there were 11 clubs: Booth came back, Blakeboroughs moved to Yorkshire Central League and Northowram Methodists joined.

| | |
|---|---|
| 1949 | 12 clubs: Siddal came back |
| 1950 – 1951 | 14 clubs: Blakeboroughs came back and Websters joined |
| 1952 – 1953 | 16 clubs: King Cross and Mytholmroyd Methodists applied successfully to join |
| 1954 | 20 clubs: more of that in a moment. |

This expansionist era was brought about under the aims of the League to provide good cricket and good sportsmanship combined with perfect support from the clubs and their representatives. The clubs decided at the 1952 AGM to expand to two divisions in 1954. Clubs were to be asked to apply. This debate lasted over 2 hours, the meeting closed at 10.10pm with representatives exhausted. The big question to be solved was how to play games in 1953 due to expansion to two divisions in 1954. After a number of amendments agreement was reached with each club playing 10 clubs twice. This was carried: 13 votes to 10. The key issue being that some clubs would have to forfeit some of their normal derby matches but it was pointed out that this would not be an issue when the clubs were placed into two divisions in 1954.

In May 1953 the Executive Committee introduced ground inspections. Clubs were inspected in 4 areas, wickets/outfield/dressing accommodation and other amenities.

Clubs and individuals were awarded prize money. In 1953 it was £1 for winning bowling, batting, fielding and wicket keeping and clubs received 5 pounds 10 shillings for winning their respective Leagues.

In 1953 clubs wanting to join had to apply by 19 September. This resulted in 4 clubs applying: Blackley, Bradshaw, Hebden Bridge Salem and Warley. The President justified the expansion, stating that it would give the new clubs impetus to keep on improving and improving. He made reference to 3 previous clubs, Stones, Booth and Barkisland all admitted before the War, all of them having improved their grounds and were now equal to the best.

The plan was to make the grounds of the League a pride to the Town and a joy to ourselves. There was, however, a slight worry from the officials that 40 years after forming the League;

could the same situation arise as in 1913/1914 when, due to the Halifax & District League's plan to revert back to two divisions it resulted in the formation of the Halifax Parish League. The worry was emphasised as like in 1914, of the 4 clubs still with the League, Triangle, Stainland, Greetland and Siddal – 3 of those were again placed in the 2nd division. So the opinion was expressed that they did not do what their forefathers had done. These fears were unfounded and the 4 clubs, Blackley, Bradshaw, Salem and Warley were admitted to form a League of 20 clubs.

1st Division: Barkisland, Booth, Copley, Dean Clough, King Cross, Mytholmroyd, Mytholmroyd Meths, Sowerby St. Peters, Stones Methodists and Triangle.

2nd Division: Blackley, Blakeboroughs, Bradshaw, Greetland, Northowram, Salem, Siddal, Stainland, Warley and Websters.

Another precedent was set in 1954 when Halifax Rugby League Team reached the Final. All the 2nd XI fixtures were moved from the 24th April to midweek 18th/19th May.

The winners of the respective divisions were:
1st – Mytholmroyd and Greetland
2nd – Barkisland and Blakeboroughs

The 20 clubs continued for a short period of stability until 1959. The only casualties being Blakeboroughs who withdrew at the end of 1956 being replaced by Bridgeholme for their first time.

In 1959 Old Town and S.B.C.I. joined to make the number now 22.

The League then remained from 1959 consistently at 22 through to 1974 when there began a movement to move to 24 – forming two divisions of 12. In 1978 shortly after this was achieved, 2 of the 3 remaining big works named teams folded: Websters in 1979 who folded just before the season started and Crossleys Carpets at the end of 1980 when the firm was taken over by Carpets International.

It was 1983 before 24 clubs were back in place with RAFA and Union Croft coming in. This number was maintained through to 1995, with Southowram replacing RAFA in 1989. Consistency, stability and well established are words to describe those 12 years with no changes except the formation of a Sunday Section in 1985.

Then in 1995 Siddal, one of the founding fathers folded. They had been struggling for a number of years prior to this.

The last of the very famous named clubs, Mackintosh's, folded before the 1996 season began, due to all support from Nestle being withdrawn. Now their ground is a nationally supported model racing circuit venue with a junior football pitch across the hallowed square.

Augustinians and Salendine Nook Old Boys replaced these two clubs, so by 1998 the League was again back to 24 clubs.

It is pleasing to comment that the values first introduced of improvement in all areas, better cricket facilities and playing better cricket have always been at the forefront of monitoring clubs. These practices were the reasons the League became attractive to clubs beyond its normal boundaries when we came into this present century combined with the fluctuating problems of how some leagues were being run.

This demand in the main came from clubs that Peter Davies has described in the book as 'Towards Bradford'. In reality it was clubs from the Bradford Central League who were seeking better cricket and playing on good grounds with very good facilities. Does it sound familiar?

The first club to make the move was Thornton in 2003 which meant an odd number of 25, so applications were sought to increase to 28 clubs with a Premier Division and two 1st Division Conferences playing an inter divisional match each week.

Oxenhope and Denholme Clough were voted in with King Cross who switched from the Central Yorkshire League for 2004 season.

However, in 2005 Salendine Nook Old Boys unexpectedly pulled out of the League, resigning at the March League Meeting, so back to 27.

For 2006 applications again were sought, but only Jer Lane were accepted taking the number back to 28. Conferences were scrapped and three divisions of 10, 8, 10 introduced. However, the clubs that were rejected were asked to improve certain facilities with a view to their applications being considered for 2007. The clubs then having complied with the League's wishes were duly elected and so Clayton, Shelf and Low Moor, who were applying for the first time, making the League consist of 31 clubs. The 3 Divisions were now formed as follows: 12 clubs in the Premier, 8 in Division 1 and 11 in Division 2. This format proved very successful with the middle division sides playing each other 3 times and proving to be very competitive with 4 clubs moving out at the end of the season.

In 2009 Wibsey Park Chapel were admitted, playing at the famous old Park Avenue ground and that made the number of clubs up to 32 with 12 clubs in the 2nd Division and no blank weekends.

Before 2010 began Halifax (ex Mytholmroyd Methodists) folded, so back to 31 and then before 2012 began King Cross folded after an Emergency Meeting was called by the club to discuss their future. Nobody was prepared to fulfil positions so despite having more than 20 at their meeting the decision was taken to disband the club.

So, now back to 30 with the clubs playing 4 teams 3 times to make a 22 match season in Division Two. Not ideal but yet again something that had been done on a regular basis in the early years of the League.

That brings us to 2014, we are still at 30 clubs with the unfortunate demise of Augustinians at the end of September 2013, having no available ground due to their current landlord, the Huddersfield YMCA not allowing cricket to be played there anymore.

Two clubs had applied to join but only one was voted in, but this voting took place long before Augustinians pulled out, so Cullingworth will become the 58th club in 100 years to play cricket in our League. At the April 2014 League meeting the application of Upper Hopton was voted on and they were voted in by a significant majority so they will join the League in season 2015 and become the 59th club to be a member of our League.

So, summing up, the growth and expansion of our League:

| Decade | Number of clubs | Decade | Number of clubs |
|---|---|---|---|
| 1910's | 7 to 10 | 1920's | 10 |
| 1930's | 10 to 14 | 1940's | 10 to 12 |
| 1950's | 12 to 20 | 1960's | 20 to 22 |
| 1970's | 22 to 24 | 1980's | 22 to 24 |
| 1990's | 22 to 24 | 2000's | 24 to 32 |
| 2010's | 30 to 31 | | |

Never been less than 7 (1916).
Never been more than 32 (2009).

It took 40 years to double in size.

It took another 50 years to grow by another 50% to 28 in 2004.

5 years further on another 4 clubs to 32 in 2009 and currently back to 30 in 2014.

Leagues, as I have highlighted, will always lose clubs for a variety of reasons but equally, providing the product on offer from that League is proven to be one that adheres to standards and is well run, then clubs will be attracted to join or in some cases re-join.

The Halifax Cricket League has always valued the communities that are at the very heart of our clubs, has put commonsense in place when acting on issues but above all, continues to provide a quality game of cricket. I believe our League over the years has earned respect from our neighbouring Leagues and is well placed to continue for another 100 years. The Executive, backed by the clubs, have in the current development plan the option to expand the League to a maximum of 36 clubs. This will only be done if the clubs applying meet all the required criteria.

We have just launched our new website on the 4th March 2014 and this has been well received by the clubs.

Our next main event is the publication launch of this, our Centenary Book, which has been compiled by our very own Peter Davies and myself, with a little help from his friends.

The book will be published on the 9th May at the Shay Stadium in Halifax when we have as our special guest, Matthew Hoggard (ex England and Yorkshire CC).

I hope you have gained some insight into our League from this brief history and I will sign off with this saying:

**"Ask not what your cricket club can do for you,
ask what you can do for your cricket club."**

*Written and Compiled by David Normanton*
*President Halifax Cricket League*
*March 2014*

# VJW Holistic Therapies

Balancing the body's natural energy
through massage and the power of touch

# Professional Massages & Organic Facials

Why not take advantage from our inspiring range of treatments, you're bound to relax and feel fully pampered.

Our wide range of massages and holistic therapies make the perfect gift for that someone special, or better still, why not treat yourself!

Gift vouchers are available on all treatments.
Prices include postage.

Wellington Mills, Plover Road, Lindley,
Huddersfield, HD3 3HR
Tel: 01484 485321
Visit us online at: www.vjw-holistics.co.uk
Email: contact@vjw-holistics.co.uk

Booking by Appointment (open Mon - Sat)

## Treatments
- Aromatherapy Massage
- Swedish/Holistic Massage
- Deep Tissue Massage
- Sports Therapy Massage
- Hot Stone Therapy
- Reflexology
- Indian Head Massage
- Holistic/Organic Facials
- Organic Body Treatments

# Presidents Past and Present

## Halifax Cricket League Presidents - The First One Hundred Years

When the League was founded in the summer of 1913, few could have imagined that for the first hundred years the office of President would be dominated by four men; Harold Clark, Harold Whitehead, Roy Smith and Terry Wynne.

In the spring of 1914 any joy as the first matches were played in the new League soon turned to horror as in August England went to war with Germany. This led to many difficulties for the whole League organisation including the position of President which changed hands several times until the mid 1920's.

There have been ten Presidents throughout our existence and Mr. J. A. Shuttleworth of Stainland was the very first League President. He was, according to the local Halifax Courier & Guardian, a very ardent supporter of the game locally and had been for a long time. He had also occupied the Presidency of the Halifax Parish Challenge Cup Competition Committee, and so had a strong connection with local cricket. Mr Shuttleworth was President from 26 August 1913 to 13 November 1913 - only about 3 months. He had decided to launch a new business venture and thus taking a practical course of action compelled him to resign from office.

The office was offered to his fellow club member Mr. J. E. Shaw. He accepted with pride and promptly donated a trophy for the 1st XI competition. At the November 1915 AGM he opened the meeting with the following sad words "The war has played havoc with our clubs and their members, naturally the call of the country comes first and we hope the allied armies will eventually come home victorious."

However in the following year another new President took office called Mr. J. Clarkson of King Cross. He was effectively President for only one year with the League suspended in 1917 & 1918. To give you some idea of the pedigree and gravitas of this cricketing chief at that time I refer to an event in 1933, when King Cross erected a new scorebox in memory of James Clarkson. Mr Bairstow, the then President of King Cross, said the scorebox has been erected by the club in memory of one of the greatest cricketing families in the District and everyone appreciated the work which the Clarkson family had done for local cricket. Please note that at the time Mr Clarkson was President, King Cross were never members of the League. It is probably another indication of the difficulties of war but highlights the determination of the League to carry on even in the severest of circumstances.

In 1919 he handed on to Mr. John Joshua Fielden of Greetland who remained President until 1928. This excellent cutting taken from the Halifax Courier (see over) gives you all the detail about this man.

The man who took over and became one of its longest serving Presidents was Harold Clark.

He was already President of Mytholmroyd and an early order 1st X1 batsman. Harold would steer the League through the late 1920s, 30s and the 2nd World War until 1946. In the 1930's the League was buying some English made leather cricket balls stamped HCL for 10s.3d. (51p) each which would be £28 at today's value but the League's financial position was very poor and by the end of 1938 the total funds were down to £2.8s.10d (£2.44).

## HALIFAX CRICKET LEAGUE PERSONALITIES.

No 1.—J. J. Fielden (Greetland).

In a few short paragraphs each week the writer intends to go the round of the clubs which at present comprise the Halifax Cricket League and pick out for review some outstanding personalities, hoping by this means to draw greater attention and create greater support for the League, out of which many local clubs have progressed into higher spheres. Many might say that it is not as strong to-day as it has been, but those who follow the League's fortunes and its standard of play closely, know differently. Amongst those who are working to attain a higher status for the League is the subject of our review.

Mr. Fielden has been connected with the Greetland club since 1910, when, after spending his boyhood days in Halifax and his early cricketing days with Brunswick Sunday School in the Amateur League, and later having a spell with King Cross (he lived only a stone's throw from the ground), he was transferred by the B.D.A., for whom he worked in Bradford, to their Greetland branch. He commenced immediately to play with the local club and was quickly elected treasurer.

The following season (1911), as captain, he led his side to victory in the final of the Parish Challenge Cup at Thrum Hall, when Clifton were defeated by one wicket, after a match which will always stand out in Mr. Fielden's memory. He filled many offices at Greetland, and was club representative on the League Committee, which comprised at that time, Sowerby Bridge, Siddal, Illingworth, Elland Edge, Greetland, Triangle, Stainland, Norwood Green, Mytholmroyd, and Lightcliffe.

On the formation of a new League on August 26, 1913, he was elected vice-president, which office he held until 1916, when the war suspended all activities. Upon resumption in 1919, Mr. Fielden was the first president, and held that office for 11 years, and he has since been elected a life vice-president. He has served his own club well, too.

President in 1921, he saw the building of the present pavilion. The ground also was purchased and extended during this time to embrace the tennis courts and bowling green, for which effort more than double the amount of money necessary was raised locally.

Outside cricket, Mr. Fielden has been a member of the Greetland Urban District Council for a period of 12 years, including three years as chairman, and he is also a member of the local joint committees and at present chairman of the Education Committee of that Board. His views on cricket are well known. Cricket is only a game, but worth playing for itself alone. Let it be said of any cricketer, " He always played cricket," and even when playing days are done let the lessons of the cricket field never be forgotten. Help also to foster the same spirit in the younger generation by devoting time to the organisation side of the grand old game. Whatever the future may hold for the League, its status can never be questioned as long as it contains personalities like Mr. Fielden, who will always be looked upon as a pioneer of real amateur cricket, and one worthy of respect from all with whom he has come in contact or who have experienced that influence of good sportsmanship which he stands for first and foremost.

—THIRD MAN.

## Death, at 71, of a former Greetland councillor

### MR. J. J. FIELDEN

A former chairman of the old Greetland U.D.C., Mr. John Joshua Fielden, of Scarr House, Spring Lane, Greetland, died at his home, to-day, aged 71. He had a long record of public service.

When a member of Greetland Council, he also served as chairman of the Greetland and Stainland Education Sub-committee, and on the Joint Hospital Committee. From the amalgamation with Elland, in 1937, Mr. Fielden represented Greetland Ward until his retirement through ill-health in March, 1946.

Mr. J. J. Fielden.

He was elected chairman of the Elland Education sub-committee at its first meeting in 1937.

For three years he was chairman of the council's Public Lighting Committee. From 1941 to his retirement he was vice-chairman of the Finance and General Purposes Committee, and served as a representative of the council on the North Dean Wood Trust up to 1943, on the Calder Assessment Committee, and as a school manager. For a year he was on the Ashlar Division Education Executive.

### METHODIST WORKER AND CRICKETER

Mr. Fielden played in Sunday School cricket in his youth, and for a few years was a playing member and committee member of King Cross Cricket Club. Later he joined Greetland Cricket and Athletic Club, captaining their team in 1911 when they won the Parish Challenge Cup.

He held office in the Greetland club, from first joining, as treasurer, and then as president for 24 years, until retiring in March, 1946, when he was made a life member. He was president of Halifax Cricket League for ten years.

While living in Halifax, Mr. Fielden was connected with Brunswick Methodist Church, where he held many offices, including that of trustee. In Greetland he had been a member of Thornfield Methodist Church. A lifelong Liberal, he had been president of Greetland Liberal Club.

Until retiring at the beginning of 1943, Mr. Fielden was cashier of the Greetland Dyeing Company, Ltd., for nearly 40 years.

He leaves a widow and three daughters.

---

The Second World War from 1939 to 1945 took its toll with 2nd XI cricket being suspended and by 1943 when Booth resigned because it's field had been dug up for the war effort, the League had reached its lowest position since 1920 with only 9 clubs, each with one team.

At the end of the war Harold Clark gave up the office of President because of ill health and the League began to look for a strong character to take it forward. The man chosen was Harold Whitehead of Stones who was the youngest President and he would hold office for 18 years until 1964.

Harold became a Head Teacher and was not afraid to take tough decisions. His strong leadership was needed to take the League forward both in terms of rule changes, expanding the League to 20 clubs with two teams each, and creating four divisions. He was well connected to the county scene which led to a number of Yorkshire stars attending League dinners, where Harold always said grace in Latin.

Harold was a good all rounder, even captaining the League representative side and he became a Stones CC hero playing a vital part in the Parish Cup Final in 1954. Stones beat Northowram Hedge Top in a low scoring match at King Cross. Harold contributed 41 runs in a Stones total of 116 and then combined with Dan Hamer to dismiss Northowram for 104. In the same season Stones finished runners up to Mytholmroyd in the League. Harold was also Chairman of Stones from 1947 to 1952 and then President from 1953 to 1975.

Harold Clark

Harold Whitehead

In 1964 Harold Whitehead gave up the office of League President and was replaced by Neville Crossley of Greetland. Neville Crossley had previously held both the position of League Treasurer and then League Secretary for many years. He is remembered as a good batsman and was always a true gentleman both on and off the field. However in 1970 Neville was forced to resign because of ill health.

The man who became the next President in 1971 was Roy Smith of Copley Cricket Club. He was a stalwart of the club and a member for 70 years. As a player Roy was a top quality wicketkeeper and aggressive opening batsman. He won the club fielding prize no less than ten times, a club record and claimed the batting prize on seven occasions. He was Copley Chairman from 1955 until 1965 when he became Club President and remained in this position until his death in 1997.

Roy's contribution to local cricket was immense and he had great influence throughout the whole area. During his leadership, the League began to establish itself in a Yorkshire context and he became well known in Yorkshire County circles. He was also responsible for establishing the Halifax Junior Cricket League.

Roy was an inspirational character to generations of local cricketers and supporters and he is remembered as a cheerful and sporting gentleman. In Halifax he was known as "Mr. Cricket"; in Yorkshire he was known as "Mr. Halifax".

Roy Smith

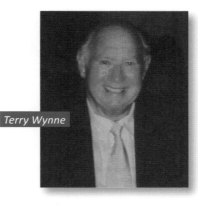

Terry Wynne

Another great servant of the League was Terry Wynne who became Chairman in 1978 and then succeeded Roy Smith as President in 1988. Terry was a playing member of Bradshaw C.C. for over 20 years. He retired in 2003 and became a Senior Life Vice President. Terry devoted many hours of hard work to uphold the standards of our League and was recognised throughout Yorkshire for his dedication to cricket by holding many offices, some of which were Chairman of the Halifax and Huddersfield Area Council, Chairman of the Collinson Memorial Committee and member of the Yorkshire Cricket Association, becoming a Life Member in 2007. He was also awarded the Halifax Evening Courier Sports Council Award for Sport and was the winner of the inaugural Yorkshire Cricket Board OSCA, (Outstanding Service to Cricket Award) in 2008. Sadly, Terry died in January 2010.

The man chosen to become the new President, proposed by Terry Wynne, was David Normanton, who would lead it to its centenary season. David, like many of his predecessors before him, had held several League Officer positions as Junior League Treasurer, League Press Officer and League Treasurer covering over 13 years.

David is a lifelong member of Stones Cricket Club and is their current Treasurer. He was until recently, a regular playing member, only retiring at the end of the 2011 season after 44 years. He had a reputation as a solid opening batsman and an excellent wicketkeeper, winning the 2nd XI League wicketkeeping prize on four occasions, the last of these being in 2010 when he was also awarded the Halifax League Umpires Annual Trophy for Outstanding Contribution to Cricket. David has also appeared in two Crossley Shield Finals, winning on the first occasion and runner up in the second.

In his ten years in office David has presided over numerous changes in the administration and organisation of the Halifax Cricket League including the original website, the new website, electronic communication, revision of the Handbook, monthly Executive Meetings and the expansion of the League into three divisions both at 1st XI and at 2nd XI.

The tradition of dedication and service of his predecessors has been continued by David as he strives to maintain the high standards of our League. He also hold apposition on the Yorkshire Cricket Board Leagues Committee and is the Chair of the West Yorkshire West Area Cricket Council. Recently the Yorkshire Cricket Board commented that "The Halifax Cricket League is one of the best organised in the whole of the County," a great tribute to David and all of his fellow officers. The future of our League is in safe hands, as David leads it forward into its second century.

*Written & researched by Tony Heptinstall*

# Reflections of Past Secretaries

## "There is a widely held and quite erroneous view that cricket is just another game."

*Duke of Edinburgh*

Cricket is interwoven in the landscape around us and plays a huge part in the social fabric of our area.

On my regular short walk I see many of our grounds from the viewpoints on and around Albert Promenade, SBCI, Sowerby Bridge, Sowerby, Old Crossleyans, Copley, Greetland and the long view through to Luddendenfoot and Booth.

During the period that I was Secretary of the League between 1987 and 2009 we lost very valued member clubs of our League in Mackintosh's, Siddal and Barkisland. The social fabric was changing and from a tight knit Halifax community, the ease of travel and the state of flux in other leagues in the area, including the demise of The Halifax Amateur Cricket Association, meant that The Halifax Cricket League grew numerically and spread its boundaries by the addition of Union Croft which became Queensbury, Thornton, Augustinians, Jer Lane, Shelf, Low Moor, Wibsey Park Chapel, King Cross, Clayton, Denholme Clough and Oxenhope.

In the summer of 1987 I first met Terry Wynne, our President who gave so much to our League. He was the man who showed me that the game of cricket was more about giving to others than it was about our achievements on the field. He was the man who taught me that cricket was above all a team game and that we are all valued individually as members of that great family of cricket lovers that is the Halifax Cricket League.

On that day in July 1987 I was playing for Sowerby Bridge and we were into the second innings at Barkisland and I was sitting alone on a bench along the top side of the ground, sulking because I had not been given the chance to bowl as many overs as I thought I should, when this chap came alongside me and sat down. He began straight into a conversation, coming to the point. "We want a Secretary" he said "to take over from Stanley Hirst. You have been recommended to me. I know you are a busy man but I want you to do the job." The rest, as they say, is history.

It is lovely to reminisce and memories are lasting and wonderful. But for me as an administrator cricket is about the here and now and our plans for the future. It's about making enjoyment of the game possible for as many people as possible. Whether you are nine and starting your first game with some other lads in a coaching session or if you are 90 and love sitting enjoying watching a game in peaceful surroundings, it is up to us as administrators to make that happen.

When I was still Secretary I received a lovely letter from Nick Lawson, a cricket Fan from Leigh on Sea in Essex. He wrote "I know there are some lovely grounds which I would love to go to sometime. I am sure you will agree that you can't beat stumbling across a nice rural cricket ground on a sunny day. Watching a game of cricket is a wonderful pastime."

Brian Laycock (ex Fixture Secretary) always said  said "Cricket is more than a game: it is a way of life."

I now keep my connection with cricket and our League by umpiring regularly on Saturdays.
I would like to conclude by congratulating the League on its Centenary and expressing the hope that, guided by the Executive under the fine leadership of President David Normanton, it may continue to thrive in the future.

*Leyland Smith*

## Mike Sheppard - Fixture Secretary 1980-2005

In August 1979 Roy Smith came up to me and said "a busy man is a contented man" so will you take over from Jim Stott.  I asked Carol and she said "what's another job" and I stood for election.

In 1980 there were 23 teams, 38 umpires a minimum of 20 overs from 6:30pm, scoring 5 points for a win, 4 points for a tie, 3 points for team scoring most runs and 1 point for team with least. The first team batting having 50 overs maximum.

A year later Crossleys resigned leaving 22 teams and sixes were brought in for the first time, much to Triangle and Batsmen's delight.

In 1983 RAFA and Union Croft joined the League giving 2 divisions of 12 teams, and a further 2 divisions for their second teams.  A Fixture Secretary's delight 1v10 2v9 3v8 4v7 5v6 11v12 with reverse fixtures for their second teams.

In those days cricket started when football finished, no overlap, Cup and Shield matches played on Sundays

In 1985 the Sunday League started which had its own fixture secretary thank goodness.

In 1989 RAFA resigned and Southowram came in. 90 over games started, 6 points for a win.

Around this time clubs were talking about altering the Bank Holiday fixtures which were at the time Derby games. This  brought me into conflict with my great friend, 'Mr Sowerby' Donald Hoyle, he considered they should play either Triangle or Stones depending which division they were in as usual on the Saturday and Monday home and away.  But the clubs voted the Derby games out, but Donald and I remained friends.

In 1995 we lost Siddal and in 1996 Mackintoshes, but in 1997 the league allowed in the first Kirklees team Augustinians and a year later Salandine Nook Old Boys (SNOBS).  Bonus points were also adopted.

In 2001 Barkisland left the league to join the Huddersfield League, and Bridgeholme returned to the fold.

In 2003 the League accepted the second Bradford club, Thornton giving 25 clubs.
In 2004 three clubs were accepted, King Cross, Denholme Clough, and Oxenhope giving 28 teams and the Conference was formed.

To a fixture secretary this formation caused many complications, A computer expert was called in and after a great struggle fixtures for the season 2004 were finalised. And a donation was given to the expert for his time. Further complications arose when Augustinians asked for a clear date to accommodate a music festival on their ground.

On a personal level I have always believed you must put back what you have taken from a sport and after winning every League medal first and second teams, Crossley Shield winners but my main disappointment was not having won a Parish Cup Winners medal, only a runner up medal. Proud to play for Sowerby during the 1962 and1963 season being the only team at the time to win second and first division titles in successive seasons. Blackley being the second team to complete the feat in 2008 and 2009.

I am also pleased to say that I have played and worked with Barry Tennyson, Tony Heptinstall and Brian Laycock on the executive committee who have put back much more than they took out.

## Contribution from Richard Davies
## An Umpires View

Cricket historians will rightly attach no importance at all to the "Courier" scorecard of the game between Booth 2nd XI and Warley 2nd XI on the last Saturday of the 1979 season. R. Davies b A. Greenwood 27. This marked the end of a wholly unremarkable career in local League Cricket - thereafter I would be an umpire.

Over the last thirty years plus I have continued to enjoy cricket, but from a different point of view. Crossley Shield and Parish Cup Finals have been special days, but perhaps I could reflect on some of the less obvious considerations which spring to mind when our weekly appointments are published.

We cannot choose which games we are given, so the standard of cricket we see being played varies considerably. In my experience this has risen for two particular reasons: many of the best players remain loyal to the Halifax Cricket League and do not try their hand elsewhere, and the grounds and wickets are being prepared to a much higher standard. A total of, say, 200 runs in the first innings, which would once have been a matchwinner on most occasions, is still competitive but frequently overtaken nowadays.

Umpires and players have their favourite grounds, though their choices will be based on different criteria. Old Town, Luddendenfoot and Booth are my top three with such wonderful views, and Triangle and Oxenhope are not far behind.

In any season we can expect some fairly challenging conditions, and in such circumstances Queensbury, Blackley, S.B.C.I. and Denholme Clough may not be the best places to be. Triangle, Warley and Bridgeholme are, by comparison, quite sheltered.

And then there are cricket teas! Through force of circumstances these were pretty average during my playing days, but the standard has been transformed. Clubhouse kitchens are now commonplace, and a wonderful spread is usually provided. Newcomers like Thornton and Jer Lane have helped to demonstrate what can be done and the tea interval is eagerly anticipated by players and umpires alike.

New clubs have been made welcome over the years, but we sometimes remind ourselves of those that have been lost. I have counted seven, of which Siddal (with more than their fair share of colourful characters) and Mytholmroyd Methodists (a village team personified) are particularly missed.

Forty plus years of happy memories - and you haven't seen the back of me yet!

*Richard A Davies*

# Snippets from the Early Minutes

**1914**    Joining fee – 2 Guineas Ten Shillings and 6d

Ovenden - landlord trouble led to Elland Edge being invited.

First Dinner - Tuesday 21st April at Heyworth's Cafe in Southgate Halifax.

The standard of the League hopefully leads to a great future!

27th October 1914 - First Annual General Meeting

**1915**    Dispute over 1 run – Greetland 72, Clifton 71. No ball not recorded was problem

Reps discussed and agreed a tie.

Lost Clifton Britannia, Sowerby Bridge and Siddal down to only 7 clubs.

9th November 1915 – Second Annual General Meeting.

**1920**    Norland not accepted due to there being the most difficult ground to get to.

**1921**    League Handbooks were introduced

**1923**    April - Each club levied 10s 6d to cover expected loss. Finances not good covered by clubs each electing a vice president to the League.

**1924**    Late starts Mytholmroyd at Turner & Wainwrights and Copley at Norwood Green, both due to the exigency of the train service (need or demand).

Stainland given permission to move match on 12th July to 6th September – due to Gala.

Norwood Green 2nd XI players did not obey umpires. Norwood Green found guilty and ordered to pay all Siddal's expenses. Game was counted as a draw.

**1926**    Changed name to Halifax Cricket League.

**1928**    'Smoker' held – the League ran an annual social evening and smoking concert at the Upper George Pub. A 'smoker' was a live performance of music before an audience of men who smoked all evening.

**1934**    Cricket balls purchased from Beecrofts at 10s/3d each – Wisden Grade A – stamped HCL.

July - Halifax League - v - King Cross (Yorkshire Council League) at Thrum Hall – proceeds for benefit of Maurice Leyland, Yorks CC – total £3/4s/0d

**1935**    New rule – side batting first must declare their innings after 2hrs 25mins. Side batting second maximum batting time 2hrs 20mins. If start delayed then umpires to adjust so that side batting second had 5 mins less time than side batting first.

**1935**   Treasurer demanding clubs pay their insurance premiums.
April – Umpires conference held. Various points appertaining to the game were raised and discussed. Prompt supply of teas at the interval was an issue put to clubs.
Copley and Clifton 2nd XI's allowed to play Whit Tuesday morning.
Matches rearranged to different dates throughout these early years seemed to cause no problems at all.

**1936**   21st season of actually playing – deemed that the League attained its majority.

**1939**   Season closed with outbreak of War.

**1940**   AGM held on Saturday afternoon at 2.45pm on October 26th.
Reported most teams maintained but failed to do justice.
League Meetings well attended characterised by good fellowship and mutual respect.

**1941**   Copley and Norwood Green could not raise teams but remained members by paying Vice President subs.
However, Booth, Dean Clough, Greetland, Sowerby, Stainland, Triangle, Barkisland, Mytholmroyd and Stones all managed two teams.
League subs were £2.

**1942**   At May League Meeting umpire reported for taking up his duties on the field of play wearing a black bowler hat. This procedure was deemed to be at the very least undesirable. Umpires secretary undertook to take up the matter.
League invited to send young players to cricket coaching at Thrum Hall.
Stones, Barkisland and Mytholmroyd clubs reported names of players who would attend.
Last match of the season between Mytholmroyd and Blakeboroughs was to decide Championship. Blakeboroughs did not raise a side, they were fined, match awarded to Mytholmroyd who were then Champions.

**1943**   Booth's field ploughed up.
Geoffrey Teal took Chair of Meeting – first time a Chairman was used.
August 28th – Stainland - v - Stones – Stones did not turn up due to excessive rainfall. No play had been possible in any of the matches. Stones fined to pay both umpires 15s/1d in total.
Officers were awarded grants: £8 – Secretary, £1 – Treasurer, £1 – Publicity Secretary.

**1944**     Army XI – 105 Military Convalescent Dept, Ovenden Park Camp, Halifax.
Sept – Clubs agreed rules needed to be completely reworded but to be left because of uncertain times.
The League reported 15 umpires, 7 unattached.
October - Mr Clark resigned as President due to ill health. Resignation not accepted.
New office of Chairman now made official.

**1948**     Rules not to be revised until clubs could be expected to adhere to them and the League could enforce them. However, there was a definite need of a revision of the rules governing cancellation so clubs agreed for a rule revision to proceed.
Stones in trouble again – did not attend and had not sent in results causing concern to the man covering cricket in The Courier. Stones still had not responded at next Meeting.
League contributed to Red Cross and St. Johns Ambulance.
First Hon. Life Vice President – Mr J H Taylor.

**1946**     'Smoker' revived in autumn at Griffin Hotel.
Len Hutton – Yorks & England
Ken Fiddling – W/K Yorks
A Duckman – Yorks County Area Rep
All attended to mark Mr Taylor's 30 years as Treasurer.
Attendance was very good with the accommodation being tested to the utmost.
Executive criticised for not bringing forward rule recommendation.
April – Meeting transferred to Plummet Line
May – Complaining to MP about cost of balls

**1947**     Rule revision approved 'en bloc'
July – provision of bells at all clubs to warn players to cease practice before start of game.
President proposed a 3rd team division.

**1948**     Executive Committee – 4 Officers, President, Chairman, Secretary and Treasurer plus 3 Reps from clubs on an alphabetical basis each year. Barkisland, Booth and Copley provided the first 3.
Applications from 3 sports clubs turned down.
Feb - Annual Dinner - Guest was Maurice Leyland. Collinson Cafe used but due to Ministry of Food restrictions no meat was able to be provided.
March – All clubs to bring in a list of registered players. 40 handbooks supplied to each club at a cost £1 each.
August - Halifax League played Bridlington Town CC. Gave a good account of themselves with Bridlington commenting that it was the finest opening batting seen all season. Halifax League 193 – Bridlington 172/9. Record gate receipts for Bridlington. Match ended at 7.20pm

Oct – Northowram Methodist's, Salem and Mytholmroyd Methodist's turned down for 1949. Grounds are to be visited with a view to expansion in 1950.
November – President proposed inviting 4 current Yorkshire Council Clubs who had been former members of the Halifax League back in 1950. Chairman Mr Teal against it!

**1949**     Played Huddersfield League at Siddal on August 24th. League team selected by a North v South match so they had a good idea what talent was available. The President Harold Whitehead was the captain of the side.
Hot debate took place on actions of players refusing to leave the wicket when given out. No concrete proposals were forthcoming on how to improve the situation!

**1950**     3rd party Indemnity Insurance approved.
2nd Teams to provide a home umpire.
Collection to be taken at all League matches for the Len Hutton Benefit Fund.
Appealed to the local paper the Halifax Courier for better coverage. One match to be featured each week please.

**1951**     League season to be 22 matches commencing on 21 April with matches at Whitsuntide plus 2 evening matches and the season ending on 01 September.
At AGM – King Cross and Mytholmroyd Methodist's admitted on a one year trial.
Umpires wanted an increase in fees from 7 shillings and 6 pence to 10 shillings. Unsurprisingly the motion was lost.
Norman Yardley is to be guest speaker at the Annual Dinner.

**1952**     Playing 20 matches starting 26 April to 6 September. Decided by 14 votes to 4 to play 5 clubs twice and 10 clubs once. Clubs to play on Whit Monday & Tuesday.
Secretary raised matter of buying a Typewriter owing to the growth of the League clerical work. The cost would be £21 which was half the balance of funds. Progress won and the motion was carried.
Umpires fee upped to 10 shillings from 7/6. There was a shortage of umpires.
Incident at Barkisland v Stones 2nd XI match where the umpire Gledhill pulled up the stumps without consulting anyone first. Why? Deemed to be dangerous bowling.
Green Final publication did not give cricket a square deal.
December – Heated discussion on how to play games in 1953 due to expansion to two divisions in 1954. After a number of amendments it was agreed to play 10 clubs twice based on positions in the League table at the end of 1952. Carried 13 votes to 10. Clubs would have to forfeit derby matches an issue that would occur in 1954 when moving to two divisions.

**1953**  Extraordinary meeting held on 10 February to divide into 2 divisions. Proposed by Siddal seconded by Dean Clough that top 8 would constitute 1st division and the bottom 8 the 2nd division. Any new applications would change this, with the new applicant being placed in division two and clubs promoted to division one.

April – Mytholmroyd Meth's game v Triangle 2nds on Whit Monday to start at 10.00am.

May – Executive Committee to introduce ground inspections using the following criteria – Wickets/Outfield/ Dressing Room Accommodation and Other Details.

September – rules drawn up for 2 division split. 2nd teams to play reverse fixtures of 1st XI team.

October AGM – expansion encouraged as admitting new clubs gave them impetus to keep on improving and improving

**1954**  AGM – Secretary Neville Crossley hails two divisions a success with no major difficulties. 20 clubs was deemed to be ideal. Promotion & Relegation had added interest and improved crowds. Stones should have done the double. They won the Parish Cup but in the Championship they lost their last match to strugglers King Cross and Mytholmroyd beat Copley to snatch it at the death.

President stressed the every club must do its utmost to improve grounds, amenities and playing strength.

November – Brian Close presented prizes at the Annual Dinner

When you read through the Minutes you soon realise that the issues you are dealing with at League Meetings today, are very similar to issues dealt with by previous Officers and representatives. I hope you have enjoyed those snippets from the first 40 years and it has given you, the reader, an insight into the administration and aims of the League. All the topics covered are as relevant today as they were back in time. I am sure the League has fulfilled many of the aims and sentiments of those early pioneers and will continue to do so in the future.

*David Normanton – President Halifax Cricket League*

# Pictorial Memories 1890's to 2010's

# 1890s

Halifax Parish Cricket Challenge Cup

A Report

on the various

Cricket Grounds

in the

Parish of Halifax.

*1891 Grounds Report*

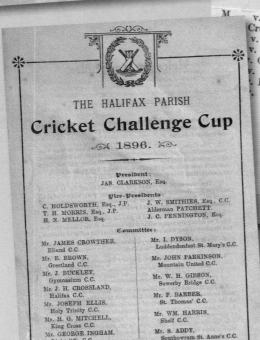

## HALIFAX PARISH CRICKET CHALLENGE CUP.

### Draw for Season 1891.

**May 30th, 1891.**

| | |
|---|---|
| Elland Tradesmen v. St. George's | A |
| Copley v. Ripponden | B |

**June 6th.**

| | |
|---|---|
| Siddal United v. All Souls' | C |
| A v. Triangle | D |
| Illingworth St. Mary's v. Skircoat Green | E |
| B v. Ovenden Albion | F |
| Lightcliffe v. St. John's Wesleyan | G |
| Clark Bridge v Police | H |
| Dean Clough v. St. Thomas' | I K |
| Lord Nelson v. Greetland | K |
| Salterhebble v. Bradshaw | L |
| Mountain v. Holy Trinity | M |

**June 20th.**

| | | |
|---|---|---|
| M v. C | | |
| Cross v. E | | N |
| v. Elland | | O |
| v. Sowerby Bridge | | P Q |
| Queensbury | | Q |
| v. Halifax | | R S |
| Hebden Bridge | | T |
| D | | U |

**July 4th.**

| | |
|---|---|
| P | V |
| N | W |
| R | X |
| Q | Y |

**July 18th.**

| | |
|---|---|
| V | AA |
| X | BB |

*1891 Parish Cup*

## THE HALIFAX PARISH
## Cricket Challenge Cup
### 1896.

**President:**
JAS. CLARKSON, Esq.

**Vice-Presidents:**

| | |
|---|---|
| C. HOLDSWORTH, Esq., J.P. | J. W. SMITHIES, Esq., C.C. |
| T. H. MORRIS, Esq., J.P. | Alderman PATCHETT. |
| H. N. MELLOR, Esq. | J. C. PENNINGTON, Esq. |

**Committee:**

| | |
|---|---|
| Mr. JAMES CROWTHER, Elland C.C. | Mr. I. DYSON, Luddendenfoot St. Mary's C.C. |
| Mr. E. BROWN, Greetland C.C. | Mr. JOHN PARKINSON, Mountain United C.C. |
| Mr. J. BUCKLEY, Gymnasium C.C. | Mr. W. H. GIBSON, Sowerby Bridge C.C. |
| Mr. J. H. CROSSLAND, Halifax C.C. | Mr. F. BARBER, St. Thomas' C.C. |
| Mr. JOSEPH ELLIS, Holy Trinity C.C. | Mr. WM. HARRIS, Shelf C.C. |
| Mr. H. G. MITCHELL, King Cross C.C. | Mr. S. ADDY, Southowram St. Anne's C.C. |
| Mr. GEORGE INGHAM, Lightcliffe C.C. | |

**Hon. Treasurer:**
Mr. C. E. FOX.

**Secretary:**
Mr. J. EDGAR CROSSLEY,
90, Park View, Halifax.

Pearson Bros., Printers, 28, Crown Street, Halifax.

*1896 Parish Cup*

# 1900s

## BALANCE SHEET, 1903.

| RECEIPTS. | £ s. d. |
| --- | --- |
| Balance from 1902 ... ... ... | 31 3 1 |
| Six Entries for 1903 ... ... | 3 3 0 |
| Thirteen Entries for 1904 ... | 6 16 6 |
| Gate money at King Cross ... | 2 0 0 |
| „ „ Mytholmroyd ... | 6 10 1 |
| „ „ Final at Halifax ... | 13 3 1 |

| PAYMENTS. | £ s. d. |
| --- | --- |
| | 1 10 0 |
| Stationery and Printing ... | 2 15 10 |
| Expenses at King Cross ... | 3 6 8 |
| „ „ Mytholmroyd | 6 0 10 |
| „ „ Halifax | 0 10 8 |
| Advert. for Entries, 1902 ... | 0 7 6 |
| Cup Insurance ... ... | 13 4 0 |
| Medals ... ... ... | 0 18 2½ |
| Postages... ... ... | 3 0 0 |
| Secretary ... ... ... | |
| Balance Yorkshire Penny Bank (Interest to add) ... | 30 0 0 |
| „ in hand ... ... | 1 2 |

| | £62 15 9 | | £62 15 |

Audited and found correct,
C. E. FOX,
H. HUSTWICK.

*1903 Parish Cup balance sheet*

## HALIFAX PARISH
## Cricket Challenge Cup.

*Halifax, 21st October, 1908.*

Dear Sir,

An Extraordinary General Meeting will be held on Wednesday evening, the 28th October, at the Upper George Hotel, at 7-30, when the Draw for Season 1909 will take place.

The above will be followed at 8 o'clock by the Annual General Meeting, at which the Balance Sheet will be presented, and the Officers for next season's competition elected.

Two Representatives from each competing Club will be allowed to attend.

Your attendance is requested.

Yours truly,

H. HUSTWICK,
Secretary.

*1908 Parish Cup letter*

*1906 Illingworth St. Mary's Parish Cup winners*

# 1910s

PARISH LEAGUE LEADERS.

## Illingworth's Success.

## The "Courier" Cup.

The Illingworth St. Mary's Club are once more to be congratulated on their success in winning the competition in the first season after peace resumption. They have had a splendid team, and the result is well merited. The Booth and Greetland clubs were healthy rivals, but, as will be seen from Saturday's results, failed at the last hurdle. The Illingworth club have still one match to play, with Stainland, but this will not effect any material difference in the League table. The whole of the clubs have done fairly well when one considers the winners have only got 9 points and the bottom club 4 points.

There is still one interesting contest to be played. There have been no second team matches, and a knock-out competition for their trophy (the handsome "Courier" Cup) is to be started on Saturday. The tit-bit for the first round will be at Greetland, where Illingworth are the visitors, but all the matches should be most interesting.

### HALIFAX PARISH CRICKET LEAGUE.
### Results Up-to-date.

| | P | W | L | D | Pts |
|---|---|---|---|---|---|
| Illingworth St Mary's | 15 | | | | 9 |
| Booth | 16 | | | | 8 |
| Greetland | 16 | 8 | 4 | 4 | 8 |
| Siddal United | 16 | | 3 | | 8 |
| Mytholmroyd | 16 | | | | 8 |
| Norwood Green | 16 | | | | 7 |
| Triangle | 16 | | | | 7 |
| Halifax Baptists | 16 | | | | 5 |
| Stainland | 15 | 4 | 10 | | 4 |

### SATURDAY'S RESULTS.
Halifax Baptists v. Norwood Green.
Ovenden. Norwood Green: W

*1913 Parish League*

## Cricket.
### HALIFAX PARISH LEAGUE.
#### FIRST TEAMS.

| | P. | W. | L. | D. | Pts |
|---|---|---|---|---|---|
| Norwood Green | 18 | 13 | 5 | 0 | 13 |
| Sowerby Bridge | 17 | 13 | 2 | 2 | 13 |
| Clifton Britannia | 18 | 12 | 4 | 2 | 12 |
| Illingworth St Mary's | 17 | 10 | 6 | 1 | 10 |
| Lightcliffe | 17 | 9 | 8 | 2 | 9 |
| Stainland | 17 | 7 | 8 | 2 | 7 |
| Triangle | 18 | 5 | 12 | 1 | 4 |
| Greetland | 18 | 4 | 12 | 1 | 4 |
| Siddal | 18 | 4 | 13 | 1 | 4 |
| Elland Edge | 18 | 3 | 13 | 2 | 3 |

#### SECOND TEAMS.

| | | | | | |
|---|---|---|---|---|---|
| Sowerby Bridge | 18 | 13 | 3 | 2 | 13 |
| Siddal | 18 | 13 | 3 | 6 | 13 |
| Norwood Green | 18 | 12 | 6 | 0 | 11 |
| Stainland | 18 | 11 | 7 | 0 | 11 |
| Greetland | 18 | 8 | 10 | 0 | 8 |
| Lightcliffe | 18 | 6 | 12 | 0 | 6 |
| Illingworth St. Mary's | 18 | 7 | 11 | 0 | 7 |
| Triangle | 18 | 5 | 12 | 1 | 5 |
| Elland Edge | 18 | 5 | 12 | 1 | 5 |
| Clifton Britannia | 18 | 3 | 15 | 0 | 3 |

All Saturday's matches abandoned owing to rain.

MATCHES & UMPIRES FOR SATURDAY NEXT
Rearranged Matches (First Teams).
Stainland v. Sowerby Bridge—Umpires from Illingworth and Siddal.
Lightcliffe v. Illingworth—Sowerby Bridge and Elland Edge.
A League meeting will be held at the Upper George Hotel, Halifax, to-morrow (Tuesday), at 7.30 p.m.

*1914 Parish League tables*

## LIST OF UMPIRES.

| Barkisland C.C. | L. Lumb, School Green, Barkisland. |
|---|---|
| Clifton Brittannia C.C. | Jas. Wilkinson, 110, Thornhill Rd., Brighouse. |
| | Wilson Jagger, New Road, Woodland, Clifton, Brighouse. |
| Elland C. Upper Edge C.C. | W. Cockshott, Calder View, Upper Edge. |
| Elland C. & B.C. | Dick Williamson, Quebec Street, Elland. |
| | Friend Walton, 22, Brooksbank St., Elland. |
| Greetland C.C. | A. Crossley, 23, Rochdale Road, West Vale. |
| Halifax C. & F.C. | Frank Thomas, 13, Parliament St., Halifax. |
| | Jas. Roberts, 6, Gaygills Terrace, Halifax. |
| Illingworth C.C. | J. W. Woodhead, Violet Street, Hanson Lane, Halifax. |
| | Jas. Chapman, Binns Terrace, Ovenden. |
| King Cross C. & B.C. | E. Abbey, 16, Eldroth Mount, Halifax. |
| | E. Crossley, Hornby St., Fenton Rd., Halifax. |
| Lightcliffe C.C. | F. Hoyle, Ripley Street, Lightcliffe. |
| Mytholmroyd C.C. | W. Heap, 4, Bridge End, Mytholmroyd. |
| | Harry Greenwood, Bank Buildings, Hawksclough, Hebden Bridge. |
| Norwood Green C.C. | G. Blamires, Bramley Lane, Hipperholme. |
| | Sam Sprockly, Edward Street, Waring Green, Brighouse. |
| Ovenden C.C. | B. Hinchliffe, 18, Forest View, Ovenden. |
| Sowerby Bridge C.C. | T. Wright, Hill Crest, Sowerby Bridge. |
| | W. Smith, 5, Salisbury St., Sowerby Bridge. |
| Sowerby S. Peter's C.C. | H. Whittaker, 13, Margate Street, Sowerby New Road. |
| | Fred Rushton, Gay Villa, New Rd., Luddenden. |
| Stainland C.C. | Thos. Meath, Lane Side, Holywell Green. |
| | Sam Mortimer, Brow Cottage, Stainland. |
| Triangle C.C. | J. Berry, Millhouse Cottage, Triangle. |

*1913 Parish Cup*

## THE
## Halifax Parish
## Cricket Challenge Cup.
### 1913.

#### President:
J. A. SHUTTLEWORTH, Esq. (Stainland).

#### Vice-Presidents:

| | |
|---|---|
| J. E. SHAW, Esq., J.P. | C. E. FOX, Esq. |
| C. H. WALLER, Esq. | W. H. GIBSON, Esq. |
| H. H. WALLER, Esq. | H. SAGAR, Esq. |
| H. BINNER, Esq. | J. HOLDSWORTH, Esq., J.P. |
| J. CLARKSON, Esq. | C. V. WRIGHT, Esq. |
| H. WHITWORTH, Esq. | T. STANDEVEN, Esq. |
| H. E. CROSSLEY, Esq. | R. STANLEY BATEMAN, Esq. |
| A. CRAPPER, Esq. | R. RAMSDEN, Esq. |
| J. LUMB, Esq. | A. ASPINALL, Esq. |

#### Representatives:

| | |
|---|---|
| Barkisland C.C. | H. N. MAUDE, Oakles House, Barkisland. |
| Clifton Brittannia C.C. | SAM BERRY, 4, Albert Street, Clifton, Brighouse. |
| Elland C. and B.C. | DICK WILLIAMSON, Quebec Street, Elland. |
| Elland Upper Edge C.C. | JAS. W. BARKER, Ridge View, Upper Edge. |
| Greetland C.C. | M. CROSSLEY, Chapelside, Greetland. |
| Halifax C. & F.C. | FRANK THOMAS, 13, Parliament Street, Halifax. |
| Illingworth C.C. | C. PICKLES, Keighley Road, Illingworth. |
| King Cross C. & B.C. | B. PICKLES, 25, Thrum Hall Lane, Halifax. |
| Lightcliffe C.C. | W. ASPINALL, East Street, Lightcliffe. |
| Mytholmroyd C.C. | J. H. TAYLOR, Mytholmroyd. |
| Norwood Green C.C. | G. BLAMIRES, Bramley Lane, Hipperholme. |
| Siddal C.C. | TOM WHITELEY, 9, Exeter Street, Salterhebble. |
| Sowerby Bridge C.C. | H. ACKROYD, Willow Street, Sowerby Bridge. |
| Sowerby St. Peter's C.C. | J. H. HOPKINSON, Haigh Farm, Sowerby. |
| Stainland C.C. | J. A. SHUTTLEWORTH, Oak Terrace, Stainland. |
| Triangle C.C. | Mr. E. BUTTERWORTH, 31, Triangle, nr. Halifax. |

#### Auditors:
Messrs. C. E. FOX and H. BINNER.

#### Hon. Treasurer:
Mr. J. A. CROWTHER, 55, Hollings Mill Lane, Sowerby Bridge.

#### Secretary:
Mr. HARRY HUSTWICK, Wrigley, Illingworth, Halifax.

# 1920s

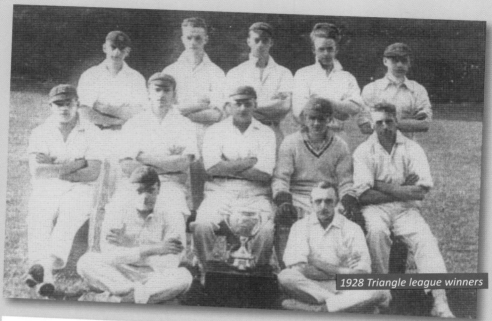

*1928 Triangle league winners*

*1929 Greetland*

## THE HALIFAX DAI[LY]

### Sport and Pastime.

**HALIFAX PARISH CRICKET LEAGUE**
League table up to May 21:—
First Teams.

| | P. | W. | L. | D. | Pts. |
|---|---|---|---|---|---|
| Elland A | 6 | 4 | 1 | 1 | 9 |
| Greetland | 5 | 3 | 0 | 2 | 8 |
| Norwood Green | 5 | 4 | 1 | 0 | 8 |
| Mytholmroyd | 5 | 3 | 1 | 2 | 8 |
| Norland | 5 | 2 | 2 | 1 | 5 |
| Baptists | 5 | 2 | 2 | 1 | 5 |
| Northowram | 6 | 2 | 3 | 1 | 5 |
| Triangle | 6 | 2 | 3 | 1 | 4 |
| Stainland | 5 | 1 | 4 | 0 | 3 |
| St. Peter's | 5 | 0 | 4 | 1 | 1 |

Second Teams.

| | P. | W. | L. | D. | Pts. |
|---|---|---|---|---|---|
| Greetland | 4 | 4 | 0 | 0 | 8 |
| Stainland | 5 | 4 | 1 | 0 | 8 |
| Norwood Green | 3 | 3 | 0 | 0 | 6 |
| Mytholmroyd | 4 | 3 | 1 | 0 | 6 |
| St. Peter's | 5 | 2 | 3 | 0 | 4 |
| Baptists | 4 | 1 | 2 | 1 | 3 |
| Northowram | 5 | 1 | 3 | 1 | 3 |
| Norland | 5 | 1 | 4 | 0 | 2 |
| Triangle | 5 | 0 | 5 | 0 | 0 |

Saturday's Results.—First Teams: Triangle 96, Stainland 62; Northowram 74, Norland 51; Baptists 19, Norwood Green 21 for 3; Elland A 247 for 8 (dec.), Greetland 194 for 7, Mytholmroyd 167, St. Peter's 129. Second Teams: Triangle 63, Stainland 64 for 8; Norland 52, Northowram 59 for 1, Mytholmroyd 91, St. Peter's 56.

Matches and Officials for Sa[turday]. First teams: Northowram v. G[reetland], umpires, Elland A and Mytholmroyd. Second Teams: Greetland v. Northowram: Baptists and Mytholmroyd. Norwood Green v Baptists: St. Peter's and

*1921 league tables*

# 1930s

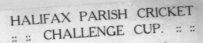

## HALIFAX PARISH CRICKET :: :: CHALLENGE CUP. :: ::

*November 8th, 1930*

The ANNUAL GENERAL MEETING will be held at the Corporation Arms, Gibbet Street, Halifax, on Tuesday Evening, November 18th, 1930, at 7-45 p.m.

Two Representatives from each Club are allowed to attend this Meeting.

### BUSINESS.

1. Minutes of last General Meeting.
2. Correspondence.
3. Report and Balance Sheet.
4. Draw for Season 1931.
5. Election of Officers.
6. Any Other Business.

JOHN CROSSLEY,
*Hon. Sec.*

1930 Parish Cup

### HALIFAX CRICKET LEAGUE

## OFFICIAL HANDBOOK

Rules, Fixtures, and Umpires, SEASON 1936

PRICE TWOPENCE

*Halifax Printing Works, George Street.*

1936 league handbook

1938 Stones Parish Cup winners

## The Halifax Daily Courier & Gu

### SPORTS EDITION

SATURDAY, AUGUST 6. 1938.

### Parish Cup Final

The Mayor (Ald. F. Watkinson, J.P.) presenting the Cup to the Stones C.C. captain, at "The Ramsdens," on Saturday last.

HALIFAX
CRICKET LEAGUE

Official
Handbook

Rules, Fixtures and Umpires

Season 1949

*1949 league handbook*

# 1940s

# SPORTS SUMMARY OF THE WEEK
## Remarkable Averages of Hamer and Bain for King Cross

*1940 King Cross Parish Cup winners*

THE MAYOR (Ald. G. Barker) made one of his last public appearances, before his sudden death on Tuesday, when he presented the Halifax Parish Cup to D. E. Jowitt, the King Cross captain, on Monday evening, at "The Ramsdens."

KING CROSS have a fine chance

BARKISLAND C.C., winners of the Halifax Cricket League Championship.

*1949 Barkisland league champions*

# 1950s

MYTHOLMROYD CRICKET CLUB

1st XI . Halifax League . Division 1 Champions . 1954

*1954 Mytholmroyd team photo*

F.Walton (com). W.Crowther (com). D.Nutter. R.A.Greenwood. J.Gledhill. R.S.Shackleton. J.Mitchell. F.Woods (com). K.Uttley (com).
W.H.Walton (groundsman).

J.Crowshaw. D.Rollins. K.Butterworth. F.K.Smith (captain). C.Pugh. H.Pugh. R.Holdsworth.

HALIFAX CRICKET LEAGUE

*Official Handbook*

RULES, FIXTURES AND UMPIRES

*1954 league handbook*

**Season · 1954**

*1954 Stones Parish Cup winners*

# 1960s

HALIFAX
CRICKET
LEAGUE

Official
Handbook

Rules, Fixtures
and Umpires

SEASON
1965

*1965 league handbook*

*1968 newspaper report*

# TRIANGLE'S TITLE BY TWO POINTS

## Division One

TRIANGLE are champions of the Halifax Cricket League. They made sure of the honour by defeating Warley on Saturday in the last match of the season to finish two points ahead of Greetland, who beat Crossley's.

Crossley's will now drop into Division Two for next season along with SBCI.

Mackintosh's made sure of promotion from Division Two by beating re-election applicants Siddal.

Dick Rodger, with an unbeaten 50, and John Charnley, with five wickets for 34, took the individual honours for Triangle, who dismissed Warley for 96.

Full details of last weekend's matches are:

**BLACKLEY v NORTHOWRAM**

Northowram won by two runs

Northowram 148.— D. Jackson c Greenman b Jagger 0, A. Butterworth c Moorhouse b Hey 58, B. Dickinson run out 2, A. Oaks b Boyne 8, H. Andrew b Greenman 50, R. Pollard c Bottomley b Boyne 0, T. Tennyent c and b Boyne 5, V. Barber b Hey 50, T. Barber c Hey b Greenman 2, F. Stennett not out 0, A. Horsfall lbw b Hey 2, extras 2. Bowling: D Moody 4-0-33-0, G. Hey 14-4-28-5, K. Jagger 8-2-25-1, D. Boyne 6-1-27-3, Moorhouse 4-0-15-0, F. Greenman 3-0-18-2.

Blackley 146.—J. Moorhouse c Pollard b V. Barber 14, K. Jagger c and b Stennett 4, W. Bottomley c Pollard b Stennett 14, D. Gaines b V. Barber 2, R. Ham b V. Barber 5, J. Wilson lbw b T. Barber 55, D. Boyne c Dickinson b Stennett 15, H. Aspinall lbw b T. Barber 4, F. Greenman not out 34, C. Hey b V. Barber 0, D. Moody b V. Barber 8, extras 6. V. Barber 10-0-55-5.

## With the second teams

**MYTHOLMROYD II v BRADSHAW II**

Bradshaw won by 106 runs.

Bradshaw 115 (only ten men); J. Haley b Crilley 15, R. Habler b Thompkins 7,

Mytholmroyd II 5-0-55-1, T. Leach 10-2-21-4. F. Garbutt 6-2-13-1.

Stainland 149 for six.—J. Lewthwaite 5, Parry 48, C. Noble c and b Parry 5, R. Lowe c and b Hamer 61, J. Holroyd

## Division Two

**BRADSHAW v MYTHOLMROYD**

Bradshaw won by seven wickets.

Bradshaw 130 for three.—K. Hubbard b Wheelhouse 20, J. Abson lbw b Sutcliffe 42, D Evans b Durgan 9, T. Ryan not out 33, R. Wade not out 17, extras 7. Bowling: Sutcliffe 10.1-0-30-1, B. Greenwood 3-0-25-0 G. Durgan 3-1-16-1, K. Wheelhouse 3-0-17-1, F. Greenwood 6-0-21-0, I. Astin 2-0-14-0.

Mytholmroyd 129 (only ten men). S. Sutcliffe b Cardwell 4, B. Lord lbw b Priestley 45, J. Astin c Chambers b Abson 18, B. Greenwood c Priestley 0, Dyson 0, K. Wheelhouse b Hubbard 45, F. Greenwood c Evans b Cardwell 4, G. White lbw Cardwell 4, G. Durgan b Abson 2, V. White b Hubbard 0, J. A. Sutcliffe not out 4, extras 7. Bowling: K. Hubbard 7.5-5-22-3, J. Cardwell 12-5-23-3, Abson 11-4-52-2, D. King 3-0-19-0, J. Dyson 5-0-10-1, G. Priestley 6-1-16-1.

**SIDDAL v MACKINTOSH'S**

*Booth team photo*

# 1970s

1973 Copley Double winners

**COPLEY FIRST XI PARISH CUP AND DIV 1 WINNERS 1973**
Dennis Bowyer David Hudson Gordon Spencer Mick Doggett Brian English Ron Bellenger
Ian Ball  Colin Radcliffe  Brian Hulme(Capt)  Derek Smith  Paul Beck

1970 league tables

1978 league handbook

# 1980s

Evening Courier, Monday, August 17, 1981

# Illingworth romp home in Shield

TWO FORMER Halifax League players did the damage as Illingworth, of the Airedale and Wharfedale League, comfortably won the Crossley Shield final at Broomfield yesterday.

Graham Robinson (ex-Crossley's) took six for 38 and Trevor Whittaker (ex-SBCI) took four for 21 as Triangle were bowled out for 90.

Illingworth, who were gaining some consolation for their first team's defeat in the Parish Cup final, hit the winning runs for the loss of only two wickets, Maurice Lawton top scoring with 32 not out.

### Crossley Shield final

**TRIANGLE v ILLINGWORTH**

Illingworth won by eight wickets

**TRIANGLE 90**

| | |
|---|---|
| K. Wilson b Whittaker | 26 |
| M. Prime b Whittaker | 15 |
| B. Charlesworth b Whittaker | 2 |
| P. Madden b Robinson | 3 |
| R. Bellenger b Robinson | 14 |
| D. Heplinstall c Rawton b Robinson | 1 |
| T. Whippey b Whittaker | 4 |
| R. Ingham not out | 7 |
| R. Robertshaw b Robinson | 0 |
| G. Roder c Lawton b Robinson | 0 |
| B. Madden c Lawton b Robinson | 10 |
| extras | 6 |

BOWLING: G. Robinson 17.2-3-38-6, T. Whittaker 13-4-21-4.

A. Smith 4-0-21-0.

**ILLINGWORTH 93 for two**

| | |
|---|---|
| C. Stott b Robertshaw | 27 |
| P. Smith b Madden | 32 |
| M. Lawton not out | 9 |
| A. Palmer not out | 18 |
| Extras | 7 |

Bowling: P. Madden 10-1-23-1, M. Robertshaw 9-2-35-1, R. Bellenger 2-0-8-0, B. Madden 2-0-11-0, G. Rodger 0.2-0-8-0.

## HALIFAX CRICKET LEAGUE

LAWS — FIXTURES — UMPIRES

*Official Handbook*

SEASON 1988

---CRICKET---

# Warley lift title with double-hit

WARLEY clinched the Halifax League title with a weekend double success.

Victories against Mackintosh's on Saturday and Sowerby Bridge yesteday gave Warley their first championship win since 1978.

They went into the weekend games with a three point lead and four games to go but 16 points from two games, coupled with a double upset for second-

"He'll have his sights set on that."

Rawson was again in form with the bat yesterday. He hit 62 in Warley's four wicket win after Sowerby Bridge had been dismissed for 139. Rawson had taken five for 31 in their innings.

On Saturday, it was Harold Smith who caused the damage, as Warley bowled out Mack's for 129.

Smith took five for 51 and a half

# 1990s

HALIFAX CRICKET LEAGUE

LAWS — FIXTURES — UMPIRES

Official Handbook

1996

1996 league handbook

1995 league XI

# ANDY STEPS UP PACE

The 1991 Parish Cup final: Nigel Askham

## Glory for Bradshaw as eight-wicket Ingham knocks Triangle out of shape

BRADSHAW underlined the unpredictability of cricket to lift the Parish Cup for the second time in four years at a packed Barkisland CC yesterday.

Paceman Andy Ingham and batsman Steve Smith were their heroes but few in one of the largest final crowds for years would have given them much hope of being on the winning side at the tea interval.

On a track widely regarded as the nearest thing to a batsman's paradise the eventual worthy winners thought they had blown it when they were restricted to a below par 185 for eight.

But Ingham's superb spell of eight for 20 left their opponents in a sorry state as they were eclipsed for only 79.

"We thought we were 40 runs short of a decent total," said jubilant skipper Chris Sutcliffe.

"But we have a marvellous team spirit and that counted for a lot. Andy bowled out of his skin. He just wouldn't let up and the Triangle batsmen just didn't know how to handle him."

A disappointed losing skipper Billy Morris was forced to admit: "Our batsmen just didn't perform. It's hard to explain a collapse like that."

Extracting more life than anyone has seen on the ground for some time, Ingham was a constant menace from the moment he had Tracey Whippey caught splendidly by the unfazed Mick Turner at short leg off a full-blooded pull — albeit at the third or fourth attempt.

Garry Rodger quickly followed, trapped lbw below, and the pre-match favourites were 33 for three when an in-ducker accounted for Dave Hudson.

Lively Bradshaw made a rare slip in the field when opener Steve Frankland, who appeared to be setting himself for the one big innings his side needed, was fortunate to make his ground when a run out seemed certain.

But Ingham made sure the mistake wasn't going to prove costly as Frankland became his fourth victim with the score still on only

... est ever Parish Cup finalist at 16, provided a real breath of fresh air at the other end with a fluent 22 which belied his tender years and promised much for the future.

But with them beaten back in the nest — Turner to a superbly square leg catch by Rodger — and skipper Sutcliffe quickly treading the same path, they were looking down the barrel at 80-odd for five.

Triangle hadn't flagoured on Smith, though, who overcame a nagging back injury to play a priceless knock.

He had spectacular, if brief, support from Simon Lees in a quick-fire stand of 43 which steadied the ship and then being around intelligently to guide theres to respectability.

It at least gave his teammates something to bowl at and Ingham responded magnificently to ensure a rich peal of his side's 1988 triumph over the same opponents.

BUBBLING OVER ... Bradshaw players celebrate their Parish Cup Final triumph with club president Tommy Bamford.

### SCOREBOARD

Bradshaw won by 106 runs.

**BRADSHAW 185 for eight**

| | |
|---|---|
| M. Turner c Rodger b Turner | 29 |
| N. Barraclough c Whippey b Madden | 7 |
| S. Bell c Kershaw b Madden | 1 |
| S. Collins b Turner | 22 |
| S. Smith not out | 62 |
| C. Sutcliffe lbw Turner | 0 |
| S. Lees b Madden | 29 |

1991 Bradshaw Parish Cup winners

# 2000s

2001 Warley Parish Cup winners

The sweet taste of success ... Rob Keywood with the cup

## Rob lifts trophy after 2,000-mile trip

Story and picture:
**Ian Rushworth**

A CRICKET captain who broke off from a family holiday in Portugal to take part in a Calderdale cup final has lifted the trophy for his team.

Rob Keywood, of Warley Cricket Club, led his side to victory over Bradshaw in the Halifax Parish Cup in Sowerby Bridge yesterday.

Just hours earlier, the 40-year-old financial advisor had bid an emotional farewell to his wife Debbie and two sons Greg,

eight, and Liam, six, in Albufeira.

"Debbie and my eldest were in tears in the hotel reception," said Rob. "They just said hurry back. It was very emotional."

But his 2000-mile round trip paid rich rewards as Rob led his side to an eight-wicket win.

Rob, who jets back to Portugal

tomorrow from Stansted airport to rejoin his family, clutched the handsome three foot high trophy and said: "I'm thrilled to bits.

"You always have little doubts in the back of your mind and I'm relieved and really pleased that it has worked out so well."

The skipper played a full part in his team's success in front of a sun-baked crowd of 900, bowling eight economical overs of left arm medium pace and picking up the key wicket of Bradshaw's

second top scorer Mick Turner for 29.

However, if Warley make the final again next year and Rob is on holiday he made it clear that the rest of the team would have to manage without him.

"It was a superb day and well worth it - but I won't be doing it again! I'm looking forward to getting back to my family."

Match report - Page 14; Dates in star - Back Page

## TRINITY INSURANCE
## HALIFAX CRICKET
## LEAGUE

LAWS - FIXTURES - UMPIRES
*Official Handbook*.
**2002**

2002 league handbook

2006 Queensbury heritage award winners

# 2010s

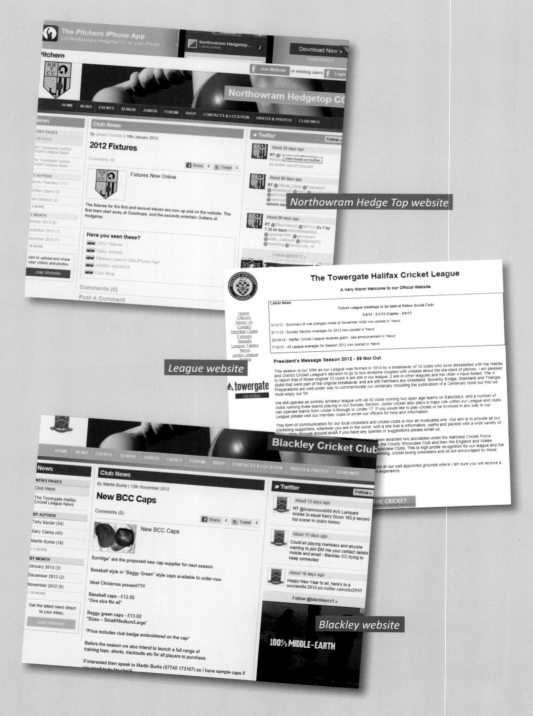

*Northowram Hedge Top website*

*League website*

*Blackley website*

# Club Histories

## SECTION 1

## Calder Valley Clubs

### Booth

Booth CC was founded in 1893. The club's debut match was against neighbours Luddendenfoot St.Mary's. Unfortunately, Booth were dismissed for just 8 runs!

In the early years of their existence, Booth were ground-less and played in various locations. These included Tommy Lane and a field behind the Woodman Inn which was also inhabited by cows.

In 1895, a pitch was levelled at Carr House. However, it seems unlikely that it was ever used as the club were offered the Woodman Inn venue, where it remained until 1942.

In 1897, the Halifax Parish Cup committee carried out a report on the grounds of competing clubs. Booth's original ground, close to the Woodman, was described as an 'irregular shape and on a fairly steep hillside.' Its dimensions were 'about 100 yards x 100 yards' with a 'laid crease 30 yards x 20 yards.'

BOOTH CRICKET CLUB.          HALIFAX PARISH CUP WINNERS 1948.

Left to right.  Seated—J. WADE, E. ELLIS (V. Capt.), R. MIDGLEY (Capt.), F. WADE, T. OGDEN.
Centre row—T. A. NICHOLL, H. V. BOARDALL, J. B. CORBOY, Coun. W. CORBOY, G. A. WOODHEAD, A. BRIGGS.
Back row—S. SMITH, D. A. DRIVER, W. E. OGDEN.

In 1900, Booth were Sowerby Division champions and in 1906 they made their first Parish Cup final appearance. During the First World War, the club was disbanded and the pioneering era of early cricket in Booth came to a close. Some of the early players moved to other clubs and others simply gave up the game.

The 1920s saw Booth get back on track. In 1921, Booth joined the Halifax Amateur League and 1927 saw them win the Hebden Bridge League. This was a major achievement as they had only joined the league in 1924.

Booth left the Hebden Bridge League in 1938 and joined the Halifax League. The club's ground had now reached the required standard for the Halifax League.

These improved playing conditions were made possible when permission to mow the outfield was gained from the farmer who owned the field. In 1943, the club felt the impact of global conflict. This time the Woodman Inn ground was requisitioned and ploughed up for food production – and used for allotments – in support of the war effort.

In 1946, permission was granted to construct a permanent headquarters at Broad Fold. Building work took place in 1947, which meant that all the club's 'home' games during that season had to be played away.

The new ground was opened on 24 April 1948, and Mr R.H.Murgatroyd, owner of the local mill, bowled the first ball on the new turf to Bob Midgley.

1951 saw Booth lose the Parish Cup final to King Cross, going down by 7 wickets. One Booth player had contracted mumps...and was therefore kept in isolation due to the rest of the team fearing for their own glands!

In 1957, the club held a special 'Booth v Booths' fundraising match. Players came from as far afield as Lancashire in order to take part in this one-off event. Via the match, a sum of £19 was donated to the Collinson Memorial Trophy competition.

The 1960s were a vintage period for Booth. They won the Parish Cup on five occasions and the Halifax League title twice. Surely this meant that Booth were the team of the decade in local cricket?

In 1950, work was carried out to reduce the slope, and in 1972 builders started on the pavilion. Forty years on, the kitchen is always busy, the walls are awash with team photos - from 1912, 1948, 1949, 1952, 1958 and later - and a blue club flag flutters from the building's roof.

There were further developments in the 1980s: the pavilion was extended, a new car park was built, and showers were installed.

Club spokesman Mike Barnett says: 'It's a small venue but very attractive. The ground is overlooked by a big manor house and, all in all, it's a lovely setting. The wicket has a tendency to keep low and I'd say that 200 is a decent par score. Our current groundsman has done a very good job.'

# Bridgeholme

There is no place called Bridgeholme, so how did Bridgeholme Cricket Club acquire its name?

The club originated directly from local industry in Eastwood, near Todmorden.

The cricket teams from Moss Brothers, Bridgeroyd Mills, and J.J.Tatham Ltd, Nanholme Mills joined forces to form one club in 1950.

The name 'Bridgeholme' was invented by combining the names 'Bridgeroyd' and 'Nanholme'. These two mills still exist today, although Nanholme is now re-named Springholme and is owned by Pickwell-Arnold.

1990 Collinson Cup winners

The club had no ground during its first season in 1951 - its only year in the Todmorden & District League - and played all matches away.

Preparation of the Station House ground on the Hebden Bridge-Todmorden road had been underway since the summer of 1952. Drainage, levelling and the laying of the square had been the priorities.

In January 1954, an application to enter the Halifax Parish Cup was rejected, in part because the ground was deemed 'unfit', yet five months later Bridgeholme were selected to host the Hebden Bridge League's knockout final between Heptonstall Slack and Birchcliffe.

Further improvements saw the club admitted to the Parish Cup and Halifax League for 1956.

Bridgeholme played their first match in the Halifax League at Blackley on Saturday 21 April 1956, losing by 45 runs.

For most of the next four decades, Bridgeholme played in the Halifax Amateur Cricket Association.

However, the resignation of Barkisland from the Halifax League in 2000 left a vacancy in that competition.

Bridgeholme applied and were willingly re-admitted. All the omens seemed right. They fulfilled all the criteria of playing on their own ground, having a good pitch and running two teams.

Bridgeholme do not have an official nickname but they are often referred to as 'Todmorden's Cinderella Club'.

The last of the town's many all-amateur clubs, Bridgeholme are somewhat dwarfed by the town's other two clubs, Todmorden and Walsden, but they now hold their own.

Also, in Keith Hudson they have one of the hardest working stalwarts in the Halifax League and in Station House one of the most attractive and well appointed cricket grounds in Calderdale.

The future looks very bright.

## Luddendenfoot

General opinion dates the formation of Luddendenfoot St.Mary's CC - predecessor club of the current Luddendenfoot CC – to some time in the 1880s. There was an obvious link with the local parish church, perhaps with a group of local choirboys.

However, local cricket historian Andrew Hardcastle has discovered that cricket was being played in the village as early as the 1860s.

In 1862, a Luddendenfoot CC played some matches in 'the meadow near the railway station, kindly loaned by Mr N.Whitworth'.

A match also took place in 1863 between Luddendenfoot Rising Star and Luddendenfoot Jolly Boys, who met in a field loaned by Mr W.H.Thompson.

These teams were no longer in existence when the current club was formed.

However, by the 1890s another local club, called Luddendenfoot UMFC, had begun to play matches at Top Shuttles, and from 1895 to 1901 appeared in the Sowerby Division League.

In 1892, the first cricket league in the Halifax area was formed. It was called the Halifax & District Amateur Cricket Association League and remained in existence until 1922.

Luddendenfoot St. Mary's took part in the first season of the competition - and were successful in the series of regionalised play-off matches which ended the season.

In 1895, the club made its first appearance in the prestigious Halifax Parish Cup competition.

Three years later, in 1898 – following on from its on-field success – St. Mary's graduated to the Halifax & District Cricket League, which contained most of the area's leading clubs.

The club had also moved to a new ground – 'The Holmes'.

On the eve of the Great War, St.Mary's joined their fourth different league competition in 22 years. This time it was a move closer to home as they joined the Hebden Bridge League.

Little is known of the club in the years after the Great War had ended. But in 1926 – the year of the General Strike – St.Mary's once again appeared in the Hebden Bridge League.

The wanderlust of Luddendenfoot St. Mary's CC was in evidence again at the end of the 1920s. In 1929, the club left the Hebden Bridge League and joined the four-division Halifax Amateur Cricket League, where it stayed until 1937.

Like many other clubs, Luddendenfoot appear to have gone into hibernation during the Second World War.

But the club was re-formed in 1949 and resumed competitive cricket the following year, joining the Hebden Bridge League.

Luddendenfoot -v- Mytholmroyd – 1980 Calder Valley Cup 2nd Team Final

Front Row : M Sunderland, M Grimley, M Cockroft, B Charlesworth, D Oliver
Back Row : D Jackson, P Swain, S Lambert, D McCoubrie, G Turnbull, S Smith

In 1950, a new pavilion was opened and three years later the ground at High Lea Green was levelled and reseeded.

By this time, Luddendenfoot St.Mary's were finding church involvement to be a major hindrance. At the club's 1955 AGM, President E.E.Cockroft commented: 'The running of a cricket club in this district...is becoming increasingly difficult'.

Until this time an individual could only become a member of the club if he or she had a connection with the church.

At the AGM twelve months later, on Monday 10 December 1956, it was decided 'to alter the name of the club...and allow unrestricted membership'.

The newly-named Luddendenfoot CC joined the Halifax Amateur Cricket Association League in 1956 and won the Second Division the same year.

In 1956, things must have been pretty desperate because, as a cost-cutting measure, the club tried to abandon their ground at High Lea Green.

By March 1958, Luddendenfoot had more cash in hand than at any time since the club re-formed in 1949, and the committee was looking to raise further funds for a new motor-cutter and new cricket tackle.

The 1960s proved to be an exceptionally successful decade for the club's 2nd XI. After the Collinson Cup had been brought to High Lea Green in 1960, the Mackintosh Cup, the 2nd XI championship trophy, was netted on six occasions between 1961 and 1970.

Luddendenfoot CC made their final change of league in 1973. This time the club joined the Halifax League, the premier local competition.

In 1984, the club made its first and only appearance in the Halifax Parish Cup final, losing to Barkisland.

It was just over 10 years before Luddendenfoot CC became established in the Halifax League and began to push for a place in the top flight. The first promotion came in 1986 when the Second Division title was landed.

In 1997, the club made further improvements to the facilities at High Lea Green by extending the pavilion. The work was made possible by a grant from the Foundation for Sport and the Arts and the new extension was opened with a match between Luddendenfoot CC Past & Present v A Calder Valley XI.

## Mytholmroyd

The origins of Mytholmroyd CC remain uncertain. However, by 1894 the club had two teams, one of which played in the Calder Valley League.

During the 1895 season, the 1st XI were joined by local rivals Mytholmroyd Wesleyan Sunday School CC in the Hebden Bridge League.

Around the turn of the century we come across the Sowerby Division League. It looks like Mytholmroyd also entered a team into this competition.

The club joined the Halifax Parish Cup competition in 1896 and were included in a grounds inspection survey carried out by the authorities.

By 1914 Mytholmroyd had joined the Halifax & District League and that year saw the 1st XI crowned champions for the first time.

The presentation of the trophy was followed by a social evening at which the 'cup was filled with a palatable beverage and the success of the club was drunk all round.'

Just after the Great War, Mytholmroyd joined the Halifax Parish League. The 1st XI won the Halifax Cup for the second time in 1923 and retained the trophy the following season.

In 1939, the club surpassed the all-round success of two years earlier. As well as winning both 1st XI and 2nd XI Halifax Cricket League titles, the Parish Cup was also claimed after the final against Triangle at King Cross.

On 25 April 1952 the *Hebden Bridge Times and Gazette* reported: 'At Mytholmroyd the field is in fine condition and once again the club is hoping to have the finest wicket in the league. There have been a few renovations made during the close season, including a new sight-board. Extensive improvements have been made to conveniences.'

In the same year, on 3 November, L.H.Parker, club secretary, announced at the AGM: 'To all former players...It would appear that to cease playing means to end all association with the club. Surely this is wrong. These are the men we look to for future guidance on committees and to give advice to the young cricketer.'

MYTHOLMROYD CRICKET CLUB

Ist XI   Halifax League .   Division I Champions ,   1954

F.Walton (Com). W.Crowther (om). D Nutter. R A Greenwood. J.Gledhill. R S.Shackleton. J.Mitchell. F.Woods (Com). K Uttley (Com).
W.H.Walton (Groundsman).
J.Crawshaw. D.Hollins. K Butterworth. F.K Smith (Captain). C.Pugh. H.Pugh. R.Holdsworth

Sunday sport was a contentious issue in the late 1950s. Sowerby Bridge District Council had emphatically refused to open its bowling greens for Sunday use, yet leisure was beginning to encroach the Sabbath.

The Halifax League was one of the first local competitions to experiment with Sunday play and it was a success.

At the Mytholmroyd CC AGM at the White Hart Hotel, Mytholmroyd, on Monday 28 October 1957, secretary N.D.Turner commented: 'During the past season Sunday cricket has been introduced and the new venture has made a substantial increase in the club's income.'

Mytholmroyd's batsmen enjoyed themselves in the summer of 1957. They struck 294 all out against Barkisland and followed that with 291 all out against Booth.

A new clubhouse arrived in 2000 – an event that acted as a spur for many other improvements and developments.

In 2002, the club organised a special trip to watch Yorkshire play in the C&G Trophy final at Lord's. It proved a successful day as the county side defeated Somerset by 6 wickets.

And in 2005, Mytholmroyd scooped the Parish Cup – a memorable achievement.

## Old Town

Old Town CC was formed as far back as 1885, although it temporarily disbanded between 1891 and 1894.

Originally, it played its home games at Middle Nook Farm on the far eastern fringes of the village. In time, the farm became the site of a house called 'Stalheim', now known as 'Burnside'.

In the early days, Old Town elevens competed in the Calder Valley League and the Hebden Bridge League, and in 1895 five members of the local Greenwood family turned out for the first team.

*The Second Eleven in the 1930's at Old Laithe*

But times were hard in 1906. In another match, Old Town came up against local rivals Cragg Vale. After travelling to the game in a specially-hired wagonette, the Old Town 1st XI was skittled out for a paltry total of 11!

In 1895, the club moved to Old Laithe, in the Chisley area. In *Old Town Cricket Club: A Short History*, this ground is described in the following terms: 'It was in a bleak and isolated position, 1,100 feet above sea level, occupying one of the last flat patches of land before the moors started. If the "Summer Game" has an unlikely home in England's climes, then at Old Laithe it was even less hospitable.'

During the Second World War, Old Laithe was requisitioned by the National Fire Service - with compensation duly paid to the club.

In 1956, Old Town Cricket Club introduced a Ladies membership category. The subscription rate was 2s 6d and in the first year 28 female members joined adding £3 10s to club funds.

The ground at Old Laithe had served Old Town well for over 50 years but in 1951 the club had the foresight to realise that its inhospitable location, 1,000 feet above sea level, would be a major handicap as other clubs improved comfort levels for players and spectators.

The club announced the formation of a special sub-committee, 'for the purpose of securing a field more convenient'. The feeling was that Old Laithe was too small and the pitch too uneven. The official history of the club says: 'Conditions were very spartan... water had to be brought to the ground for each match and toilet facilities were distinctly elementary. Something better was needed!'

In 1957, the club eventually relocated to Boston Hill.

In 1954, the *Hebden Bridge Times and Gazette* stated: 'The ground, in an ideal setting and surrounded by trees, is in marked contrast to the bleak exposed field at Old Laithe, which has the unenviable distinction of being one of the highest cricket grounds in Yorkshire.'

Boston Hill was christened on 27 April 1957, with Old Town 2nd XI taking on Stones 2nd XI.

The new ground not only hosted cricket but the Whit Monday Gala - a big local event - and various functions and dinner dances, many of which were fundraisers for OTCC.

The *Hebden Bridge Times* explained how a thunderstorm had interrupted the opening proceedings – extremely appropriate if you've ever witnessed the climactic changes on a summer Saturday at Boston Hill!

On this red-letter day, and in modest, unassuming terms, a club official described OTCC as 'a small obscure club on a remote hillside'.

Officials revealed that local farmers had loaned the club tractors, and local businesses an array of industrial equipment. The local press estimated that 'voluntary labour' had saved the club between £1,000 and £2,000.

Club spokesman Peter Sutcliffe puts the ground move into historical perspective: 'Where our current ground now stands, there was once a big house, ornamental gardens and a pond. I think that in the early 1950s the club was getting itchy feet and saw the potential in upping sticks and moving to Boston Hill.'

Old Town capped the momentous year of 1957 by winning the top-four play-off cup.

The club's first season at Boston Hill (1957) was also the last season of the Hebden Bridge League. Remaining loyal to this local league to the end, it was fitting that Old Town should win what proved to be the league's last match, the top-four play-off final against Halifax 2nd XI at Thrum Hall. Old Town, dismissed for 75, bowled Halifax out for 55.

The loss of four teams from the Hebden Bridge League in the autumn of 1957 threatened its very future and that of its remaining clubs. Although the Old Town committee was prepared to arrange friendly matches if necessary, the expenditure involved in creating and maintaining Boston Hill made competitive cricket essential and they made a provisional application to join the Halifax & District Amateur Cricket Association.

It was a wise step. The Hebden Bridge & District Cricket League, founded in 1894, had haemorrhaged clubs for the last time and was officially disbanded on 30 December 1957.

At Old Town's Annual General Meeting on 6 January 1958, president Raymond Ashworth revealed that the club had made firm its application.

Five days later, the 1st XIs and 2nd XIs of Old Town and Heptonstall Slack, the last remnants of the Hebden Bridge League, were admitted to the Halifax Association where they dominated the third division in 1958.

Old Town won the title with ease and the club's labours in preparing Boston Hill bore fruit in 1959 when, along with SBCI, they were admitted to the second division of the Halifax League.

The Boston Hill ground was crucial to Old Town's acceptance. The hard work of the members had paved the way for a new chapter in the club's history.

Men of this calibre do not allow a sense of achievement to foster complacency and Raymond Ashworth was already looking to the challenges ahead: 'We have a lovely ground, but shall have to face heavy expenditure on up-to-date equipment if we are to keep it so.'

Old Town played only one season in the Halifax Association, 1958, winning the third division.

In that season, Albert Harding achieved the rare feat of taking all 10 wickets in an innings – and they were all Old Town batsmen!

The first and second teams were in the same league and Albert's performance came in the match between the two. The first eleven were all out for 132 and Albert took 10 for 43 as the seconds were dismissed for 73.

# Sowerby Bridge

A set of 'Rules' exists which was adopted by Sowerby Bridge Cricket Club on 26 April 1852, at what appears to be its inaugural general meeting.

This club is probably the one referred to in the *History of Sowerby Bridge Cricket Club* which was published as part of the *Handbook of the Sowerby Bridge Carnival & Rosette Day* in 1925.

It played at White Windows and was disbanded some time before the current Sowerby Bridge CC was formed in 1877.

1992 flood

Rule 6 specified that 'any Gentleman desiring to join this club shall communicate his intention in writing', so membership was clearly restricted to those of higher social status.

In the period between this club being disbanded and the formation of the current Sowerby Bridge CC, cricket retained a strong presence in the town.

A group which was 'composed in the main of manufacturers' sons and of the gentry in the neighbourhood... played the game on land in the vicinity of the present Willow Park'. This team was known as Sowerby Bridge United, but was also given the nickname the 'shirtneck lot' because of their social status.

The current club was (re-)formed in 1877 and began playing on the Walton Street ground. Some of the earliest members of the club are listed in this account of its history and they included: Messrs. W.A.Sutcliffe, now of Westfield, Frank Clay, of Wood View, Hollins Lane, James Clay Horsfall, John Wood (who played several times for the county), and the late John D.Wilson, who was probably the first president.

The original club played at first at Fore Lane - between Sowerby Bridge and Sowerby - and another venue in the town, just off Burnley Road.

The club moved to its current headquarters in the period immediately following the end of the Great War, and purchased it in 1936.

The original Walton Road scorebox was erected in 1934; today, a simple scoreboard is incorporated into the frontage of the new pavilion.

During the Second World War, the Walton Street ground was used by the War Office as a detention barracks or prisoner-of-war camp.

One barracks official remembers: 'During the war I was stationed at the detention centre, where the cricket ground is now. The ground itself was tarmaced for a parade ground, and two mills on either side of the entrance housed the gym, workshop, sleeping quarters and sergeant's mess'.

Approximately 200 soldiers were held there. One morning one of them broke away and swam across the river and escaped. Someone went after him and caught up with him at the Friendly Pub.

As such, the club had to find an alternative venue for its wartime fixtures, and so it lodged temporarily at Sowerby St.Peters CC, up the hill in Sowerby village.

Because of the 'merging' of the two clubs between 1939 and 1945, when the war finally ended, some Sowerby Bridge players switched to the St.Peters club and some players from St.Peters moved in the opposite direction.

For the duration of 24 years, between 1961 and 1984, Sowerby Bridge competed in the Central Yorkshire League.

Sowerby Bridge won Division 3 of the League in 1965 – the first year it had run – under the captaincy of Brian Lawrence. They won it again, with T.Martin as skipper, in 1972 and 1973. It was decided to burn down what was left of the changing rooms. And the black smoke brought a visit from the local constabulary.

# Sowerby Bridge Church Institute

The earliest mention of Sowerby Bridge Church Institute (SBCI) CC comes in 1878 – a 2nd XI away match at Elland St.Mary's.

The cricket club was linked to the Young Men's Class of Christ Church, Sowerby Bridge.

During a financial crisis at the Institute in the early 1930s, brought about in part by economic depression, the cricket club was told it would no longer receive financial support.

The members responded by making the club financially independent from the church, and since then the club has grown apart slightly from its roots.

*1946 team photo*

The first SBCI CC fundraising whist drive and dance was held at the Victoria Assembly Rooms on 2 February 1935. The five-piece New Astoria Band was booked at a cost of 50 shillings, and a profit of £2 14s 6d was recorded.

War hit the club hard: there was no committee meeting between March 1940 and September 1941, at which point the club ceased to function and the ground fell into five years of neglect.

In the early 1950s, SBCI Under-18s dismissed Siddal for 12 - and lost the game when they were bowled out for 11, losing by one run!

After overcoming Division 1 league leaders Triangle in the semi-final, the odds were stacked against SBCI when they met Booth in the 1964 Parish Cup final. SBCI won by 1 wicket in a thrilling game.

The SBCI Ladies' Fund-Raising Committee held their first meeting on 15 January 1965 - their stated aim 'to raise money for the Cricket Club'.

Their first event was a hair-dressing demonstration, but bazaars, bring-and-buys, jumble sales and dinner dances became the annual core of their activities.

By 1970, the ladies were expanding their horizons into more social activities. A trip to Bradford to see the Black and White Minstrels was minuted as 'most enjoyable', and a raffle was held which made a profit of £1 17s.

In recent years, SBCI have been one of the most pro-active clubs in the Halifax area in encouraging women's cricket.

And the club's future was secured in 1998 when they scooped £160,000 to build a new pavilion – and also help them promote women's and youth cricket.

# Sowerby St.Peters

Local cricket historian Andrew Hardcastle refers to a team in Sowerby in 1855. There is also mention of a game between 'Sowerby' and Triangle in 1862.

According to Hardcastle, 'Sowerby' opened a new ground in 1869, 'more spacious and better adapted to the game' with a match against SBCI.

It is not clear whether any of these early Sowerby teams became 'Sowerby St.Peters CC' at a later date. All we can safely say is that cricket was played in the village at some point in the later nineteenth century.

Around the turn of the century we come across a 'Sowerby Division League', though no sign of Sowerby St.Peter's CC.

1930s team photo

The earliest record of the club's existence is a fixture card, dated 1904, which is currently on display in the club's pavilion. In this period there was also another team in Sowerby – St. Georges.

The fixture card from 1904 shows that the club's president was the Vicar of St. Peter's Church, the Reverend John Walker MA.

The church had a central role in the community and being able to play for the village cricket team made membership of the congregation an added attraction.

At this time, whist drives and beetle drives held in the school hall across the road from the church provided much needed funds for the cricket club. Another major source of money was collecting and selling old newspapers.

During the Second World War, when the War Office requisitioned Sowerby Bridge cricket ground for use as an army detention centre, the St.Peters club showed true wartime spirit by taking in their homeless rivals for the rest of the war and beyond.

They also issued a joint membership card.

Sowerby St.Peters were a force to be reckoned with in the post-war decades. In 1983 the 1st XI crowned one of the greatest years in their history by winning the Parish Cup for the second year running.

Today, St.Peters Avenue is a top-class local league ground. A visiting fan comments: 'Excellent facilities, good atmosphere and great for children. A traditional ground with a nice ambience.'

## Warley

In the early years of the twentieth century, Warley Young Men represented the village in cricketing competition.

This club was linked to Warley Congregational Church Sunday School. It appears that this club gradually became known as Warley CC.

2004 Parish Cup winners

Cup kings: Warley celebrate retaining the Parish Cup at Copley yesterday

# Midwood keeps his promise to deliver

Early Halifax Parish Cup records reveal that Warley made their first appearance in the competition in 1906, though it is not totally clear whether this was the Sunday School side or another.

In the 1920s, when the club was temporarily defunct, cricket was still played at the Paradise Lane ground.

One old photograph from the decade shows local cricketers mixing with umpires, players of knur and spell (an early form of golf especially popular in the Halifax area), and women of the village.

After a series of meetings in late 1932 and early 1933, Warley CC was resurrected.

At a meeting held on 12 January 1933, W.Moore moved, and J.G.Fawcet seconded, a proposal that 'G.H.Summersgill should meet with Mr Wilson about the field and draw up an agreement.' Many of the members worked tirelessly for the new club during this early period.

At the AGM held on 10 February 1939 it was recorded that: 'On behalf of the members of both teams Mr W.Litely presented Mr E.Copley with an electric reading lamp, in appreciation of his work on their behalf.'

Paradise Lane has seen its fair share of improvements. The original pavilion had a new floor and new roof put in, and the current construction was built by club member Howard Smith in the 1960s.

Ian Buckley is another club stalwart. As a boy during the war he acted as club scorer and played for Warley for several decades.

He has vivid memories: 'In the early days we had a problem with the grass. It was too long.'

'Sometimes you could run five for a gentle push! In the end we had to move some sheep into graze during the week - just so it would be short enough for the weekend!'

In recent years Warley have scooped silverware aplenty and the superbly named Paradise Lane stands as one of the most intimate and atmospheric of Calderdale cricket grounds.

# SECTION 2

# The M62 Corridor Clubs

## Blackley

On 7 May 1869, Blackley United played away at Elland and lost by 20 runs. Later on in the summer they visited Lindwell Victoria, going down this time by 18 runs.

There is also evidence to suggest that a group of local men each chipped in 1½d per week to get the club up and running around this time.

In the early days, 'local rules' applied at Blackley's picturesque home ground.

If a ball hit the boundary it was two; if it cleared the fence it was four. And there was no pavilion as such - just a small wooden hut adjacent to where the Golden Fleece pub now stands.
And there were tennis courts too, sited adjacent to the pub.

Blackley's first recorded game took place in June 1870, while in 1880 they moved into league cricket (possibly the West Vale League).

The club still possesses a book of minutes that stretches back to the first years of the twentieth century.

The highlights? A call for a lawn-mower price list (1903); a motion in favour of a weekly 'dancing' night in the pavilion (1904); and a suggestion to the effect that a fixture against Salendine Nook be accompanied by a garden party (1906).

In 1920, Blackley joined the Huddersfield Cricket Association League and reached the Lumb Cup final.

Later, during the Second World War, we are told that the cricket square was kept in neat condition by locals playing bowls on it!

Blackley's ground was put up for sale in 1946, and, with the club not having enough funds, Mr Fred Wilkinson, club president, bought it and drew up a 999-year lease.

In 1970, the club was informed that a section of the cricket ground was required for the new M62 slip road – a major dislocation.

Work on a new pavilion began in 1976, but was halted when a freak storm ripped the roof off the new pre-fabricated building. A 'Disaster Appeal' was launched (apparently, one local pensioner saved up £5 over five weeks and donated the money to the club!) and the appeal made the Yorkshire Post newspaper. Finally, enough money was raised, and a brick building was erected, that would not be blown down by the wind!

On the eve of the new pavilion opening, club members were devastated to learn of the death of their president and driving force in this venture, Richard Wilkinson.

On 13 August 1978 the new pavilion was officially opened by Yorkshire fast bowler Tony Nicholson and dedicated to the memory of Richard M. Wilkinson, president of the club between 1974 and 1978.

The club has never looked back since then, and now proudly boasts three open age teams, five junior teams and a ladies team. The club has twice reached the Parish Cup Final, and in 2009 finally won the Premier League Championship for the first time in its history. It is ECB Clubmark accredited and regularly hosts the prestigious Parish Cup Final, together with representative cricket matches on behalf of the county.

## Greetland

Local cricket historian Andrew Hardcastle has uncovered matches featuring a number of Greetland teams during the mid-nineteenth century, with the earliest coming in 1858.

By 1864, a team called Greetland Royal Albert was playing matches, and in that year they met West Vale United. In 1869, another local derby saw Greetland Victoria meet Greetland New Delight.

By the time the Halifax Parish Cup committee carried out a report on the grounds of member clubs in 1891, Greetland's move to West Vale had taken place.

The report explained: 'When completed, this field gives promise of being a very good one.'

In 1894, Greetland became founding members of the Halifax & District Cricket League. They also won the Parish Cup – thus becoming the first club to break the Halifax-Elland stranglehold on the trophy.

Greetland also bagged the Parish Cup in 1911.

In 1919, the club began to hold an annual Workshop Competition for local works teams and others.

During the 1920s, Greetland CC began to arrange annual away fixtures during the Wakes Week holiday.

*1975 2nd XI Division 1 champions*

One such match was played at Pateley Bridge, in North Yorkshire, where some remarkable early action photographs were taken.

A Greetland women's team also existed in the 1920s – an indication that the inter-war boom in ladies cricket affected small village clubs as well as 'town clubs' such as Brighouse and Todmorden.

1934 was a busy year for Greetland. They won the Parish Cup, they bought a scoreboard from King Cross for £18, and also A.J.Richardson was employed as cricket coach during May and June. His fee was 5/- per evening.

In the 1930s, a local blanket manufacturer, John Horsfalls (based on Stainland Road), donated the ground, The Holme, to Greetland CC as a gift. The club was charged just a pepper-corn rent - sixpence a year.

In 1957, Greetland bagged the Parish Cup and the Halifax League Championship – a very special 'double'.

As club stalwart Billy Betts comments: 'Greetland were a top side in the 1950s and 1960s'.

Recently, Greetland welcomed players from ex-Halifax Association side New Riding CC – and are looking forward to a bright future.

## Outlane

Outlane CC was formed in 1897 as Outlane Methodist New Connexion Cricket Club.

In 1898, a tent (pavilion) was purchased for £2-10-0d and in 1903 a subscription appeal was launched to pay for a new pavilion costing £18.

The 1917 season saw the cricket ground requisitioned by the wartime authorities for food production and the club effectively ceased to function.

A momentous meeting took place in April 1919 at which the club decided to 'take hold' of the field and also change its name to Outlane Cricket Club. The church trustees were also asked to renounce all claim to the club.

The club originally played their Huddersfield Association fixtures near Outlane Golf Club but in 1929 they moved to a new ground at Cote Farm, and then in 1934 they relocated to Lindley Moor.

In 1951 running water arrived and then, on 3 April 1958, the club was able to purchase the ground off Websters Brewery for £100.

The 1960s were dominated by motorway-related troubles. The first mention of the proposed M62 came in 1961, and by June 1964 the club had made its first official objections.

In 1970, the club was told to vacate their ground so building could start – and they only returned in 1974.

In between, they hired the Highfields ground in Huddersfield for home fixtures, although it was also mooted that the club might move permanently to another site, either in nearby Mount or Salendine Nook.

On their return to Lindley Moor, the club laid a new wicket and erected a new pavilion. They also had electricity and a bar.

In 1975, the 1st XI won the Halifax Parish Cup and the Under-18s and Under-14s won their respective league titles – a golden summer.

On 30 August 1997, there was a fire at the club, caused by a faulty thermostat in the kitchen. Extensive damage was caused by the smoke, which meant having to renovate the whole of the clubhouse.

In 2004, Outlane CC put on a spectacular Sportsman's Dinner at the Cedar Court Hotel, Ainley Top. The main speaker was Essex and England batting legend Graham Gooch.

# Stainland

Although local cricket historian Andrew Hardcastle has found references to cricket being played in Stainland during the 1870s, the current club traces its roots back to 1884.

By 1886, the club's fixtures and officers were being printed in the *Halifax Courier*.

Fixtures included matches against Hartshead, Outlane, Halifax St.Thomas, Elland 2nd XI, Crosland Moor, Colnebridge, King Cross, Lightcliffe, Paddock Congregational, Hopwood and Longwood.

The club also had an entry in the *Athletic News* Cricket Supplement and Directory.
For the best part of 40 years – 1884-1922 – Stainland played their home matches at Drury Lane, a venue famous for its bandstand.

PARISH CUP  STAINLAND  1973

UMPIRE
GODFREY  BRIAN  KEN  IAN  RICHARD  COLIN  LEONARD  UMPIRE
ELLIS  EVANS  HOWSON  NORCLIFFE  SEVERN  NOBLE  NORCLIFFE

TONY  DENNIS  HAROLD  JOHN
WOOF  SEVERN  JOWETT  HOLROYD  BENNY
GREEN

PARISH CUP RUNNERS UP. 1973

VERSUS COPLEY

In 1894, the club became founder members of the Halifax & District League.

Stainland enjoyed their first Halifax Parish Cup success in 1901, beating Lord Nelson by 7 wickets in a low-scoring final. Gate receipts at Thrum Hall were more than £24, which suggests a healthy crowd was in attendance.

In 1922, the club received their current ground, on Stainland Road, as a post-war gift.

The working men of the village had a new recreation area, and the folk at the British Legion were named as trustees. It was christened the Memorial Ground.

Under the captaincy of E.Longbottom, Stainland scooped the 1st XI Second Division in 1959.

1968 was also a superb year for Stainland 2nd XI. They won the Crossley Shield under the captaincy of J.Lewthwaite – and also netted the Division 2 title.

Some at the Memorial Ground argue that the club has been unlucky.

Like all local cricket clubs they have been on the lookout for young cricketing talent, but recently they have been scuppered by the fact that, for all the modern housing going up in the village, few new residents have knocked on the club's door wanting to play cricket.

In 1998, Stainland's pavilion burnt down. The council provided the club with some temporary changing facilities and a portakabin to use as a tea room, but the club had to think long-term.

They decided to go it alone, and by May 2001 a handsome new pavilion had been erected and officially opened.

## Stones

Stones Cricket Club, Ripponden, was formed through the local Wesleyan chapel. Their first ground was situated in a field opposite the church. This can still be identified today, as a ledge where the wicket was levelled remains visible.

A number of other local teams were members of the Halifax & District Amateur League in the late 19th and early 20th centuries: Barkisland, Zion, Soyland Town, Rishworth and Ripponden Conservative Club.

In the early days, Stones fielded a side made up exclusively of cricketers with the surname 'Whiteley'!

Like many other local cricket clubs, Stones were affected by the Great War, and closed down due to the dislocation. They moved to Swift Cross in the immediate post-war period.

Up until 1924 the Swift Cross ground was rented. The opportunity then came to buy the ground for £100. Four club members acted as trustees, providing £25 each. The ground was bought from J.R.Whiteley at Great House.

In the 1920s and 1930s Swift Cross was not just the site of a cricket ground; there was also a putting green and a set of tennis courts.

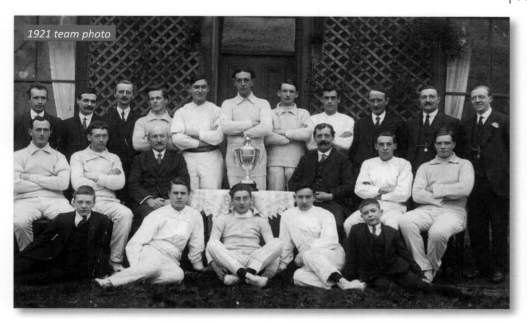

1921 team photo

Some time in the 1930s the club changed its name from Stones Wesleyans to Stones Methodists. Given that the club is now known simply as 'Stones', this means that it has had three different incarnations.

In the 1930s, members erected a small tea hut near where the scorebox stands today. They had brought the construction all the way from The Shay football stadium in the middle of Halifax.

In 1938 and 1954, Stones bagged the prestigious Halifax Parish Cup – a real achievement for a small village side.

A new pavilion was opened in 1971. In 1995 the building was extended and refurbished - the whole project costing £25,000.

And the building has been updated and extended since.

Stones recently held a fundraising Sportspersons Dinner at the Cedar Court Hotel, Huddersfield, at which England Test selector Geoff Miller was guest speaker.

And the club is proud that club stalwart David Normanton is currently President of the Halifax Cricket League.

Their home at Swift Cross remains one of the highest and most interesting cricketing venues in the area.

# Triangle

Triangle Cricket Club was founded in 1862. It was originally attached to Triangle Reading Club, which was based at the Old White Bear Public House.

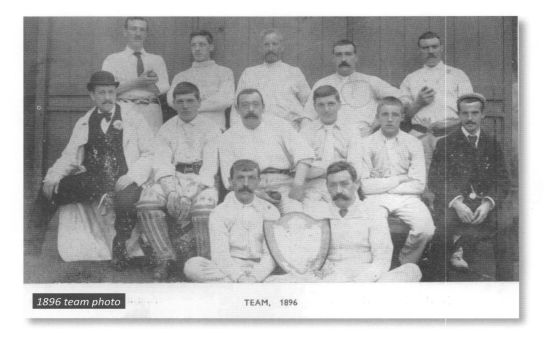

1896 team photo      TEAM, 1896

Initially, the club had 40 members. They played their first match on 20 October 1862 against Sowerby.

Grassy Bottom, Triangle's cricketing HQ, staged a special athletics event on Whit Monday, 1878.

The club won the Halifax Shield Competition twice in succession – in 1886 and 1887. In the following year, 1888, they entered the Halifax Parish Cup for the first time.

Around 1890, rugby was played on Triangle's ground. But this was brought to an end when a bank was built to allow the field to be flooded, so that skating could take place there in the winter.

Triangle bagged the Halifax Parish Cup for the first time in 1903. In the same year, Jack Steele was employed by the club as professional and captain.

In 1913, Triangle officials attended the meeting at which the Halifax Parish Cricket League was officially formed.

Grassy Bottom was bought for £650 in 1927 by local mill-owner Colonel Tom H.Morris. Morris then presented it to a board of trustees acting on behalf of Triangle CC.

Triangle scooped the Parish Cup in 1930 – beating Smith Bulmer's by a massive 96 runs – and then again in 1947 and 1953 and 1955.

In 1968, the club's 1st XI and 2nd XI both tasted success – topping their respective Division 1 tables. But Triangle lost in the final of the Parish Cup, even though they were much fancied.

The scorebox at Grassy Bottom moved in 1982 – from on top of the pavilion to the other side of the ground.

Triangle CC boasts its fair share of women members and supporters. The club also has a female secretary – Margaret Whippey. In short, women are now fundamental to the running of local cricket clubs, Triangle included.

On matchdays the club's female supporters tend to congregate near the tea hut and main entrance

And, like many other local cricket clubs, Triangle rely to a significant extent on the goodwill of local sponsors.

Grassy Bottom remains one of the most beautiful and atmospheric cricket venues in Calderdale, and in recent decades the club have claimed more than their fair share of silverware.

One club spokesman adds: 'We can safely say that no-one is still with us who witnessed Triangle Cricket Club being founded in 1862, which is a great pity because early accounts of the club are sparse and dates of events are sometimes conflicting.

'This is not unique to Triangle. The men of 1862 and the following years were not interested in history. They wanted to play cricket. These are not dusty sheets of paper but the story of cricket at Grassy Bottom.

'How many other clubs can boast a 150th anniversary? It is known that cricket was played in Triangle long before this, and there are many legends about the village cricketers playing the game in a manly fashion on Norland Moor below the Ladstone.

'Legend must not be too readily set aside, as although the passage of time and the repetition of legends by successive generations by word of mouth often changes the detail, the basic facts are generally found to be true.

'The field has a beautiful location on the banks of the Ryburn stream, being surrounded by trees, and well away from the bustle of traffic on the main road. Apart from cricket, the ground has been used for local gatherings, ranging from sports meetings of many kinds to pop concerts and Rushbearing, and it has always been valuable as a place where the inhabitants can find rest and relaxation on summer days, when it is a real suntrap.

'Many local cricketers were in their earliest days taken down to the ground by their parents, and so their earliest acquaintance with Grassy Bottom was made before they were in a position to know anything about cricket.'

# SECTION 3

# Towards Bradford Clubs

## Clayton

The club was founded in 1951 under the name of Clayton Methodists due to its church links.

Initially, the club played friendly matches and all the games were played away from home due to the pitch not being suitable to play on.

1952 saw the club play its first competitive season. Clayton Methodists were entered into the Bradford Mutual Sunday School League and played in Group 'C'.

The club's first competitive game was played at Allerton. Clayton were bowled out for a paltry 45 before dismissing Allerton for 22.

In 1954, the league expanded and Clayton were placed in Group 'D'.

However, successive promotions in 1954, 1955 and 1956 saw Clayton enter the top flight of the league in 1957. Their stay in this division was shortlived as they were relegated that season.

In 1997, Clayton moved from the Mutual Sunday School League to the Bradford Central League.

The first season saw the club find its feet in the new league with both teams finishing mid-table in Division 3. The following year both the first and second teams were Division 3 Champions and promoted to Division 2.

1999 saw the two teams promoted again, both promoted as runners-up in their respective league.

In 2000, the rise to the summit of the Bradford Central League was complete when both teams were crowned champions of Division 1, with the first team holding off a challenge from title favourites Thornton. Cup success also followed with the club achieving a cup double by winning the Waddilove and Thrippleton trophies in 2003.

It became apparent that the club needed to move leagues as the Central League was beginning to lose clubs and the club wanted to improve itself. Clayton applied to the Halifax Cricket League in 2004.

The initial application was rejected but after improvements were made to the ground with a new scorebox and improved shower room, the club was accepted into the league in late 2005 to play in the 2007 season.

## Denholme Clough

The first documented game of cricket being played at the ground on County Bridge is in 1922 when the club joined the Bradford Mutual Sunday School Cricket League (BMSSCL).

It was eight years before the club won its first honour when the 2nd XI won the BMSSCL Section 2. It was a further eight years before the 2nd XI repeated the feat of 1930 and won the BMSSCL

Section 2. The First XI's first honour came a year later when they secured the BMSSCL Group 'C' title.

Another barren spell occurred between 1939 and 1950 before the 1st XI tasted success, winning the BMSSCL Group 'B' title. They secured another title in 1957 before they left the BMSSCL and joined the Keighley & District Cricket League.

The club failed to make any impression in their new league and the struggles of the club were highlighted in the 1962-63 season when the club didn't run a 2nd XI. The start of the 1964 season saw them return to the BMSSCL, where further success was tasted by the 1st XI before the decade ended.

For the 2nd XI, their only success of the 1960s was a cup final appearance in the H.Broadbent Trophy, played at Clayton. It wasn't until 1977 that the 2nd XI were once again playing in the H.Broadbent Trophy final but as with the first final it was without success. In 1979, the 1st XI were BMSSCL Group 'C' winners and in the same year the 2nd XI made it to the cup final.

The start of the 1980s was the start of the club's most successful spell, winning eight trophies and reaching two more cup finals in a 13-year spell. The 2nd XI were BMSSCL Section 2 winners in 1981 and 1983. In 1983, the club were also winners of the West Riding Sunday Council Cricket League (WRSCCL). In 1985, the 2nd XI made their fourth cup final appearance at Salem and the club were runners-up in the WRSCCL.

The 1st XI's first cup final appearance came in the 1986 Sir James Roberts Cup at Manningham Mills. The club left the BMSSCL after the 1988 season and joined the Bradford Central Cricket League. A year later the 1st XI became Division 3 champions.

The club's most successful season came in 1993 when both the 1st XI and the 2nd XI were league winners as well as being the aggregate points winners. The club's last honour came in 1994 when they lifted the Wilkinson Sword Trophy.

In 2001, with the outbreak of the foot and mouth epidemic, the club was forced to play all of its games away from home due to the location of the ground. 'Home' games were played on Sundays at opposition grounds.

In 2003, the club took the decision to switch to the Halifax Cricket League in time for the 2004 season.

After a bright start to their time in the Halifax Cricket League, the club has since struggled. But the ground has been redeveloped and a junior section has been launched.

2009 was definitely a season of progress. The 1st XI managed to win three times, beating Queensbury, Augustinians and Stainland. The 2nd XI also had success, winning six times. The season will probably be best remembered for being the year when the water was cut off!

2009 was a strange year for results with the club having the largest losing margin and one of the highest winning margins in the same season. The 1st XI lost by 331 runs against Premier Division opposition in Mytholmroyd, before beating Augustinians by 220 runs. Augustinians were bowled out for 37, chasing 257.

## Jer Lane

The club was formed as Jer Lane Congregational Church Cricket Club in 1923. It was known as this until 1969 when it assumed it's present title of Jer Lane Cricket Club. Shortly after this the church was demolished for a development of residential property. This can be seen opposite the ground gates over Jer Lane. It was for some time a pre-requisite that only members of the church could become members of the cricket team, but this rule was gradually relaxed. Jack Watkinson, a founder member of the club, was the longest serving until he died in 1985.

The original ground was adjacent to where Whernside Mount and Jer Grove now stand.

In 1925 moves were made by the Drake and Fieldhouse families to purchase the present ground for the sum of £800, and place it in trust to ensure that cricket would continue to be played at Jer Lane. The area where the ground is situated was originally mined for coal and bell mines are still under the field albeit having been filled in.

The club was a member of the Bradford Mutual Sunday School Cricket League until 1946, when it joined the Bradford Central Cricket League.

In 1972 the club suffered a severe set back when the pavilion, which was an R.A.F. guard room was burned down, along with many of the club records. A massive fund raising effort took place to build the present pavilion which has since had numerous improvements added.

The club has won numerous honours in all manners of competitions in both senior and junior cricket. The club has also participated in the Yorkshire Champions Trophy on numerous occasions and reached the final in 1989.

In 1985 and 1990 the club have played host to Yorkshire County Cricket Club in aid of their captains benefit years. Phil Carrick and David Bairstow brought teams along to Jer Lane including Geoffrey Boycott, Arnie Sidebottom, Kevin Sharpe, Jim Love, Peter Hartley, Darren Gough to name a few. These events were a tribute to the committee and members of the club who put in so much effort in staging such prestigious events.

## Low Moor

The first recorded mention of Low Moor Holy Trinity CC was in the Bradford Observer dated 18 June 1894 when the club was all out for 32 and lost by 7 wickets. An old minute book from those early years makes interesting reading and indicates that some of the early problems were similar to those of today.

Meetings were held in the 'tent' almost every week and one of the points raised was that ground improvements were going so slowly because of the lack of support from some of the players, while team selection was questioned as to whether the best players should always be picked ahead of those who did most work.

Membership in the early 1920s was confined to those who attended church regularly and the club president was the vicar who was apparently quite a formidable character. Money raising was just as important then as it is today and a dance was held in one of the local Sunday Schools, knowing full well that the vicar did not approve of this flaunting of bodily contact! In his sermon the following Sunday, he lambasted the club from the church pulpit for this terrible sin and stood down as president. It was some years before things got back to normal.

In the early Sunday School days nobody had a car and most people worked on a Saturday morning so the matches didn't start until three o'clock and finished not later than ten past seven. Not a lot of cricket. Over the years there were spells when the club wasn't doing well and others when it won a few trophies, most famously a cup win at Bradford Park Avenue in 1975 when the winning run was scored off the last ball of the match with the last pair at the wicket.

Over many years, there have been three different grounds and the present ground was under threat from developers who were wanting to build houses there. They were managed to be put off for a few years, but without any legal rights to the lands. Eventually the club was given an area of land towards the golf course which had to be levelled and turfed, and a wicket laid.

The first match on the new field was played in April 1989 and after many years of fundraising the club was able to build a new pavilion, which was opened by the club's Senior Vice President, Mr Frank Tetley, on 8 July 1990.

The club was accepted into the Halifax Cricket League in 2007.

(Trevor Tetley - President)

# Oxenhope

Howard Smith has been involved at the club for 48 years, between the ages of 14 and 62, when he retired. He played his last game in 2011 and is now 62. He is clear about the significance of the club:

'It's a small village club with two open-age teams and five junior sides.'

'Our village is very friendly and positive about the club.'

'Most players come from the village – and there are lots of father and sons. It's definitely a family club.'

'And we've done well in the Halifax Cricket League.'

'As a club we now have several local rivals: Cullingworth, Denholme, Harden, Oakworth and Howarth, though they play in many different leagues.'

The club have played in the Bradford Central League and West Bradford League.

Their ground is on the way to Hebden Bridge and they also boast a religious link - they were once known as Oxenhope Wesleyans.

They joined the Halifax Cricket League seven or eight years ago. Smith makes some interesting points about the way that local cricket has changed: 'The wickets weren't as good decades ago. There was little knowledge and technical equipment. Huts were wooden – and these have definitely improved.

'Today we've got a very good team. Over the last 10 years we've really come on – it's been a real team effort'.

In recent years, the club has been indebted to groundsmen Ian Jowett, Ken Hopkinson and Eric Whitehead.

And in terms of cricketers, Paul Ellison has proved himself to be one of the best in the League. But it's a team effort and the club has boasted many good players.

Oxenhope, the village, is a typical Pennine community. It has lost industry over the years but has gained new housing, though the club would have enjoyed a bigger supply of cricketers!

For the most part, the club has relied on local folk who have lived in the village a long time.

The club is constantly trying to progress and recently acquired the prized Clubmark accreditation

## Queensbury (formerly Union Croft)

Union Croft Congs Cricket Club was a club that originated from Union Croft Congregational Church in Ambler Thorn. The club played in the Halifax & District Nonconformist League until 1939. This league was renamed in 1937 to the Halifax Sunday School League and then folded in 1939 due to their being only 6 clubs.

Union Croft then joined the Bradford Sunday School League for the 1940 season and remained there until 1982.
That year was a very memorable one because they did the famous double double in that League. Their first team won the League and Cup and their second team also achieved the same results.

Flush with this tremendous success on the playing front coupled with the need and desire for the club to play a better standard of cricket helped the club gain admission to the Halifax Cricket League for season 1983 along with the Royal Air Force Association (R.A.F.A.). this brought the number of clubs in the League back to 24 playing in two divisions of 12.

Queensbury Cricket Club was formed on the 1st January 2000 as a result of the merger of Union Croft CC and Yews Green CC and has no connection with the former Bradford League club of the same name.

The Club started life playing at Roper Lane before moving to Sam Lane which is now known as The Old Guy Road ground, This ground being nearly 1200 feet above sea level, is believed to be one of the highest grounds on which regular league cricket is played. On a clear day panoramic views are offered westwards down the Calder Valley to Lancashire and eastwards beyond the Emley Moor transmitter.

## Thornton

The earliest record of a match on our present-day cricket field is a game between Thornton United (an amalgamation of the local Prospect and Dole mill teams) and The Eighteen, a representation from the rest of the village, on 28 August 1853.

Friendlies continued to be played under various names until 1893 when Thornton were one of the founder members of the West Bradford Cricket League.

During the following years they moved from league to league as new leagues were formed, until after the Second World War when, from 1947 to 2002, they remained in the Bradford Central League before their latest move into the Halifax Cricket League.
The move came about due to the success the club was having on the field, especially during the 1990s and it was felt that to continue this success a new challenge was required.

A lot of the top clubs in the Bradford Central League had already left; old rivals like Harden had joined the Aire-Wharfe League, and it was felt that others would follow suit and therefore the standard would drop.

The club took the initiative and after an abortive attempt to join the Halifax Cricket League for the 2002 season, their application was accepted for the 2003 season.

# Wibsey Park Chapel

Steve Tomlinson has been involved at Wibsey Park Chapel for 25 or 26 years.

He says: 'We played in the Bradford Mutual Sunday School League, Dales Council and Bradford Central League. And then in 2009 joined the Halifax Cricket League.

'We were fed up in the Central League. We applied to the Halifax Cricket League, had to wait a year – we played friendlies – and then took our place.
'Our early years are linked to Park Chapel, a church in West Bowling that is now closed. Our players generally come from Wibsey and our derbies are against Clayton, Shelf, Queensbury, Low Moor and Jer Lane.'

Tomlinson describes the WPC folk as 'very much a team', with tea ladies Susan Fenton, Lynn Airton and Lynn Hassall 'all chipping in, with everyone contributing'.

The club was born in the late nineteenth or early twentieth century. It became Wibsey Park Chapel only recently, having been known as Park Chapel for most of its life – named after a church in West Bowling, which is now closed down.

The move to Bradford Park Avenue more than 10 years ago has worked out well. Club folk say the changing rooms are not the best but everyone is enjoying the historic, ex-Yorkshire CCC venue.

The club used to play at Haycliffe Lane, Wibsey, and their 3rd XI still play there.

The 1st and 2nd XI play in the Halifax Cricket League, the 3rd XI in the Dales Council. The club fielded no junior sides in 2003.

Park Avenue is in Little Horton, about one mile from Wibsey.

In recent years, the club has won a couple of gongs – the Terry Wynne 1st and 2nd division titles. Tomlinson continues: 'We rely a lot on cricketers from the local area. As a result, it's a healthy club.

'Les Cousins is club president. He's a significant guy. He's been at the club 50 years plus – he was a player and is now a key official.'

# SECTION 4

# Halifax Central Clubs

## Bradshaw

Although the current club was not formed until 1923, local cricket historian Andrew Hardcastle has found a number of references to clubs playing cricket in Bradshaw before this time.

The earliest of these was in 1861 when a team called Bradshaw Golden Fleece played Queenshead United.

A Bradshaw-based church team called St.John's was also active in the 1860s.

By the 1890s, Bradshaw Mills were playing in the Halifax Parish Cup competition and had joined the Ovenden & District League.

Bradshaw Cricket Club was born in 1923 during a meeting at the Bradshaw Tavern, the pub that still overlooks the ground today.

The summer of 1923 also witnessed Bradshaw's first taste of trophy success, with the club bagging the Collinson Cup.

Bradshaw decided to start a junior team in 1952 and the first junior fixtures were in 1953.

Plans were under discussion in 1959 for a pavilion to be built and fencing would also be altered.

At a meeting it was decided that the pavilion could not cost more than the £273 that was quoted by the National Playing Fields Association.

The new pavilion was officially opened on 29 May 1960.

A 15-mile walk was arranged in order to raise money for the club's memorial gates.

In September 1968, they were officially opened, a short service was conducted by the Vicar of Bradshaw, and a cricket match followed.

Bradshaw celebrated their 50th birthday in 1973 by organising a dinner at the Saxon Hotel which was attended by many ex-players.

In 1978 a Mr T.Corbett asked the club if six sheep could graze on the outfield. The club committee immediately agreed – realising that this was a means of ensuring the grass was kept short!

The Ladies Section decided to organise some social events in 1988, including an aromatherapy demonstration, a body shop evening, a reflexology demonstration and a knickerbocker clothes party!

The image of a white castle dominates the club crest - due recognition of the fact that White Castle Breweries owned the Bradshaw Lane ground in yesteryear.

Today, Bradshaw are a successful club with a beautiful ground that stands 919 feet above sea level – the highest in Calderdale.

## Copley

We are told that Copley Cricket Club (founded 1880) had a precursor in the shape of Copley United CC, who were apparently playing in 1864.

In 1891, the Halifax Parish Cup Committee appointed a sub-committee 'for the purpose of visiting and inspecting the grounds of the various clubs entered for the cup competition' so that they could: draw up a report setting forth the particulars of each ground, more especially with regard to their suitability for the playing of a cup-tie game.

Subsequently, a report was produced for each ground and Copley was described as follows: 'This field is approached by means of a footpath just below the canal from the road leading from the station to the village, 'tis about 5 minutes walk from the station. The field measures 180 x 75 yards across the centre of the crease which latter however is not in the centre of the field, but placed considerably nearer its narrow end. The crease measures 40 yards x 40 yards and is on the whole a good one, the outfield is also fair. There is seating for about 20 and two small pavilions.'

Today, the club's framed memorabilia in the pavilion bar emphasises its history, including team photos from the early twentieth century ('West Vale Baptist League Champions 1901', 'Akroydon and District League Winners 1902'...).

An intriguing document from yesteryear also hangs in the pavilion bar. A Yorkshire Federation report stated that Copley's ground covered 17,545 square yards, that motor hire cost the club £4 10s per year, and that gate fees raised £14 per annum and tea sales £18.

It was also noted that seating facilities were 'not sufficient' - a minor problem that has been well and truly rectified since.

In 1909, one of the small pavilions referred to in the 1891 report was replaced by a new building. It was opened on 1 May by the club president, Mr A.Briggs, who described the occasion as 'a red letter day' in the history of the club.

The Halifax Courier also reported that Mr Briggs described how the club had 'felt for some time that they needed better accommodation for meeting visitors and for themselves' and 'decided that when they did make the effort it should be in no half hearted fashion'.

He went on to say how 'every year sport takes a higher place in village and town life...and was one of the influences which helped elevate the tone of the people', and in view of this, it was hoped that 'for many years to come the pavilion would be used for the sport of the district'.

This final wish of Mr Briggs was more than fulfilled, as the pavilion remained in use for 60 years. Unfortunately, however, the match against Warley, which had been staged to celebrate the opening, was rather less long-lasting and had to be abandoned due to rain after two overs, with the visitors' score left at 1-0.

When the 1909 pavilion was finally replaced in 1969, the new building was positioned at the opposite end of the field. It was possible to use this former area of marshland because of the flood-prevention scheme that had been launched after the River Calder broke its banks in 1947.

The ground was bought from Bentleys Yorkshire Brewery for £200 in 1920. This was divided into an initial payment of £100 and a further £10 payable for each of the next 10 years.

Interestingly, the payments were raised solely by a specially-formed Ladies Committee, which disbanded once the transaction was complete.

Locals remember the day in 1947 when the River Calder burst its banks. Current groundsman Tom Thorpe explains: 'The ground used to get flooded, and then the whole of the village. The water just used to seep through the whole place. On one occasion some of our wooden benches were transported by the torrents onto the main road!'

Today, the venue is safe from flood alerts. Mounds have been built around the ground - and the village - to stop the spread of water, and the Water Board has made strategic adjustments to the water flow.

The floods used to affect Copley in the winter months; not in the summer, thankfully!

After Halifax (1946), Triangle (1947) and Booth (1948), it was the turn of King Cross to lift the Parish Cup in 1949. They defeated Copley in the final.

Copley's 1st XI and 2nd XI began the 1960s in wonderful style.

Brian Hulme skippered Copley to the "double" in 1973.

Ian Ball was 1st XI skipper in the mid-1970s.

In 1977, Copley won the (local) Collinson Cup and the (national) Haig Club Knockout Trophy.

Special guest John Hampshire played eight Tests for England – and after his playing career finished he became an umpire, officiating in Test matches and One Day Internationals.

Copley won the league in 2003 under the captaincy of Richard Thorpe, but just missed out in the final of the Parish Cup to the R.Keywood-led Warley side.

Copley Lane is a regular venue for set-piece Halifax Cricket League occasions.

## Northowram Hedge Top

Northowram Wesleyan Cricket Club was launched in 1919 and, in its formative years, competed in the Halifax & District Nonconformist League which, after the Great War, was reformed in 1920.

In 1926, the club moved to its current home at Hedge Top Lane, which was owned by Coley Hall Estate and gained membership of the Halifax & District Amateur League.

In 1937, the club underwent its first change of name due to the amalgamation of the Wesleyan and the Ebenezer denominations of the Nonconformist Church, and adopted 'Methodists' as their corporate title.

In 1946, when organised cricket was reintroduced after the war, the club joined the Halifax & District Amateur League, and a year later became members of the Halifax Cricket League.

The club's current name was acquired in 1952 when connections with the local Methodist church were severed because the club organised a Christmas raffle which the Methodist hierarchy viewed as 'gambling' and, therefore, unethical.

In the same year, the club purchased its ground from the Coley Hall Estate, and in 1954 Hedge Top were defeated by Stones in the Parish Cup final.

The club won promotion to the 1st Division in 1961 and caused an upset when they defeated red-hot favourites Triangle in the 1965 Parish Cup final.

The team then went on to become 1st Division champions a year later – going unbeaten throughout the season. Since that time, the club's championship record could be described as comparatively modest.

The 1st XI won the 2nd Division Championship in 1970, 1975, 1984 and 1997, and lost to Triangle in the 1998 Parish Cup Final. It did, however, win the Lindley Moor Trophy in 2003. The 2nd XI were winners of the Crossley Shield in 1971, 1987 and 2003.

## Old Crossleyans

Old Crossleyans is a relatively young cricket club, formed in 1976.

It has a historic link with what is now the Crossley Heath School, located close by in the Skircoat area of Halifax.

The Crossley Heath School is the product of a 1985 merger between Crossley & Porter School and Heath Grammar School.

Crossley & Porter School was originally the Crossley Orphanage and became a secondary school in 1919. Heath Grammar School had been founded by Dr John Favour in 1600.

Boarders at the school previously resided at Standeven House, Broomfield Avenue. What is now the function room and bar used to be the schoolboys' library.

Even though the boarders have long since gone, the school still uses the arena for sports fixtures. And today, Old Crossleyans CC play their home fixtures at Broomfield Avenue.

Old Crossleyans joined the Halifax & District Amateur Cricket Association in 1976. In the early days, they were very much an 'old boys' cricket club.
Today, Old Crossleyans are a hybrid organisation: there is a rugby union club, a cricket team, a squash side and a junior rugby league XIII. The grandiose clubhouse by the main entrance, Standeven House, serves all club sportsmen.

Not so long ago, Old Crossleyans were captained by Australian batsman Charlie Daly.

He was also involved in a special sponsorship deal, whereby the club benefited financially if he hit a certain run target by the end of the season. Daly did his bit in the nick of time - and the club duly hit the jackpot!

Old Crossleyans celebrated 25 years of cricket in 2001. To mark the anniversary, they held a special reunion event, which was attended by players from the 1970s, 1980s and 1990s and many other guests. Ex-England batsman Derek Randall was the speaker.

Today, perhaps just less than 50% of the club's members have a connection with the school. As such, it is now an 'open' club and welcomes new members from all over.

The club run a 1st XI, 2nd XI and a Sunday team, plus junior sides. Club officials also suggest that their ground is the biggest in the Halifax Cricket League in terms of the size of the playing area.

# Shelf

According to local historian Andrew Hardcastle, cricket was played in Shelf as early as the 1850s.

Shelf made their first appearance in the Halifax Parish Cup in 1896.

That year also saw the competition organisers update a ground inspection report which had first taken place in 1891.

Shelf were still playing in the field behind the Shoulder of Mutton Inn.

The ground was described as 'a large square field' which was 'evidently well looked after'. It had a 'good pavilion' and 'a little seating'.

In 1897 Shelf won the Parish Cup. The final against Queensbury was a well attended affair.

Takings for the match reached £14 11s 10d, while expenditure was £5 3s 9d, leaving a profit of £9 8s 1d.

In 1903, Shelf became founder members of the Bradford Cricket League and they hold the distinction of becoming the first ever champions of the league. In that first season only one of their 22 matches ended in defeat.

Although it is known that Shelf dropped out of the Bradford League in 1911, details of which competition the club joined have been less forthcoming.

Shelf CC seem to go 'off the radar' during the inter-war period. Details of their progress in the Bradford Central League are hazy, and they are certainly not competing in the Halifax Parish Cup.
In 1939, Shelf carried off the Bradford Central League's 1st XI knockout competition.

There was a special night in 1950 for R.J.Parker (local headmaster), Wilson Barker (grass cutter) and John H.Moore (club official and player) who were presented with club life memberships by future Ashes-winning skipper and Knight of the Realm, Len Hutton.

Between 1969 and 1974, Shelf's 1st XI scooped the Bradford Central League title on four occasions and the Waddilove Trophy once, while the 2nd XI were even more successful, winning the league championship twice and the Thrippleton Cup on two occasions.

The club juniors also won the T.Joy Cup in 1968 and 1971, bringing the club's tally to 11 trophies in six years.

The club switched to the Halifax Cricket League from the Bradford Central League.

## Southowram

Founded in 1977 and therefore much younger than most of their rivals, Southowram CC boast an idyllic ground and excellent facilities.

Southowram CC was founded by a group of local enthusiasts who had decided that it was high time a new club bore the village's name. Their base was the Cock and Bottle pub.

The new club applied to join Division II of the Halifax Association and was accepted after a re-election application by the works team Peglers was rejected.
To begin with, the new Southowram CC had no ground in the village and played its 'home' matches at Calderdale Council-owned sports pitches at Roils Head and in the grounds of Spring Hall. Second-team matches were played at Wainstalls.

One thought was uppermost in the minds of the people involved with running the new club – acquiring a home ground in Southowram itself.

Various possibilities were touted, including a field close to the parish church. But in the end an unlikely solution was found.

Ashday Lane in Southowram was the site of a former quarry. Marshalls PLC gave Southowram CC a lease on the site and the ground took shape in the early-1980s – it was levelled, covered with topsoil and then grassed.

In 1988, at the fourth time of asking, Southowram were elected to the Halifax Cricket League's

Second Division, replacing RAFA.

Then, in 1993, a new, handsome pavilion was opened – a major landmark in the club's history. In August 2000, Southowram met Outlane in the Parish Cup final at Copley and came away with a 13-run victory – another red-letter day.

The popular new Twenty20 format, which had drawn big crowds to county grounds, came to the Halifax Cricket League in August 2005 – and Southowram CC were the inaugural winners.

And then came the recent Parish Cup victory over Booth.

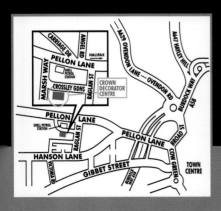

# Sunday League

## History, Officers & Honours

# Sunday League Member Clubs 2014

1. Almondbury Wesleyans
2. Barkisland
3. Birkby Rose Hill
4. Blackley
5. Bradshaw
6. Copley
7. Elland
8. Greetland
9. Illingworth
10. Lightcliffe
11. Norden
12. Northowram Fields
13. Northowram Hedge Top
14. Old Crossleyans
15. Outlane
16. Queensbury
17. Rastrick
18. Southowram
19. Sowerby Bridge
20. Sowerby Bridge Church Institute
21. Sowerby St Peter's
22. Stones
23. Thornton
24. Triangle

## Officers

**President:** David Normanton
E-mail: president@halifaxcricketleague.co.uk

**Chairman:** John Sunderland
E-mail: jbsunderland@hotmail.co.uk

**Hon. Secretary:** Gordon Akroyd
E-mail: gakroyd@sky.com

**Hon. Treasurer:** Gordon Akroyd
(as above)

**Hon. Fixture Secretary:** Simon Finch
E-mail: sundaysection@yahoo.co.uk

# Sunday League Member Clubs

**In order of first joining the League**

| | | |
|---|---|---|
| 1 | BARKISLAND | 1985 - |
| 2 | BLACKLEY | 1985 - |
| 3 | GREETLAND | 1985 - 1988, 1993 - 1994, 2000 AND 2006 - |
| 4 | HALIFAX | 1985 - 1998 |
| 5 | ILLINGWORTH | 1985 - |
| 6 | OLD CROSSLEYANS | 1985 - |
| 7 | SOWERBY ST PETER'S | 1985 - |
| 8 | STONES | 1985 - |
| 9 | R.A.F.A.(ROYAL AIR FORCE ASSOCIATION) | 1986 - 1990 |
| 10 | SOWERBY BRIDGE | 1986 - |
| 11 | UNION CROFT / QUEENSBURY (NAME CHANGE 1999) | 1987 - |
| 12 | KING CROSS | 1988 - 2009 |
| 13 | SOWERBY BRIDGE CHURCH INSTITUTE (S.B.C.I.) | 1988 - |
| 14 | TODMORDEN | 1988 - 2000 |
| 15 | SOUTHOWRAM | 1989 - |
| 16 | GREETLAND / R.A.F.A. | 1991 - 1992 |
| 17 | NORTHOWRAM HEDGE TOP | 1991 - |
| 18 | BOOTH | 1992 - 2012 |
| 19 | TRIANGLE | 1992 - |
| 20 | COPLEY | 1993 - |
| 21 | OLD TOWN | 1993 - 2008 |
| 22 | NORDEN | 1994 - |
| 23 | NORTHOWRAM / NORTHOWRAM FIELDS (FROM 1997) | 1994 -1995 AND 2010 - |
| 24 | OUTLANE | 1994 - |
| 25 | STAINLAND | 1994 - 2003 |
| 26 | BRADSHAW | 1995 - |
| 27 | RASTRICK | 1995 - |
| 28 | BRIGHOUSE | 1997 - 2001 |
| 29 | AUGUSTINIANS | 1999 - 2013 |
| 30 | LIGHTCLIFFE | 2001 - |
| 31 | MYTHOLMROYD | 2002 - 2010 |
| 32 | WARLEY | 2005 - 2013 |
| 33 | ELLAND | 2006 - |
| 34 | ALMONBURY WESLEYANS | 2012 - |
| 35 | THORNTON | 2012 - |
| 36 | BIRKBY ROSE HILL | 2014 - |

# A Brief History

Prior to 1985 a number of clubs in the Halifax Cricket League were fielding a 3rd XI in the Halifax Association. The quality of the facilities in the association were inferior to those in the Halifax and other local Leagues, and so a number of clubs formulated the idea of creating a Sunday League using their own grounds and facilities.

At the League Meeting on 03 April 1984 a letter from John Fraine (see letter on following page), the then Barkisland third team captain, proposing the formation of a Sunday Section was discussed under Any Other Business. This letter was sent to Roy Smith, the President, and is originally dated 25 August 1983. A copy had been circulated to all clubs but only 3 clubs, Barkisland, Greetland and Stones, were in favour. The matter was deferred to the June meeting. At the May meeting Barkisland appealed to clubs to seriously consider running a 3rd team in view of a number of obstacles that had been placed in the way of the current 3rd XI's playing in the Halifax Amateur Association League. The June meeting put off a decision until July, then August and then eventually it was the September meeting when the Barkisland rep Howard Cooper told the League Meeting that interested clubs had met on the 28 August with 6 clubs from the Halifax League and 5 others clubs from other Leagues. He reported that the next meeting was on the 05 September. The umpires indicated that they would not be able to provide umpires, however, it was agreed that a sub-committee be set up and they would be responsible for drafting a set of rules. In October the newly elected Secretary of the Sunday League Mr. John Stanger sent a letter to Terry Wynne the League Chairman setting out how the Sunday League would be run. The contents of this letter were strongly rebuffed by the League Executive to such an extent that the Halifax Cricket League did not want to be connected with this new venture. After much discussion between the parties, compromises were reached by the December League Meeting. Thus it was agreed at this meeting that the new Sunday League should go ahead providing the existing 3rd XI clubs playing in the Amateur League could gain clearance. These clearances were confirmed at the February 1985 League Meeting with an entrance fee set at £25 for Halifax League Clubs and £35 for outside League clubs.

Eight clubs were involved in the initial year of operation in 1985; Illingworth, Stones, Sowerby St. Peter's, Blackley, Barkisland, Halifax, Greetland and Old Crossleyans. Home and away fixtures were arranged, giving clubs 14 league fixtures together with the Courier Cup knock out competition which was played over two further rounds and a final.

As the number of clubs participating, including others from neighbouring Leagues, increased the League was divided into two equal sections playing League fixtures, with section winners and runners up, but with no promotion or relegation. The makeup of the sections was randomly determined at the beginning of each season.

In 2002, after much debate, the section was reorganised into three divisions with promotion and relegation between the divisions. The Courier Cup was renamed the Rod Warhurst Trophy in memory of the local sportsman in the same season.

In 1989 two founding stalwarts John Fraine of Barkisland and John Kenworthy of Stones gave their names to the Fraine/Kenworthy Trophy which is presented annually to the club gaining the most points over the last six matches of the season. This brought it into line with similar trophies awarded in the Saturday League and ensured that clubs always had something to play for in their final matches.

The Sunday League started with 8 clubs and expanded as follows;

| | | | | | |
|---|---|---|---|---|---|
| 1985-8 | 1986-10 | 1987-11 | 1988-14 | 1989-14 | 1990-14 |
| 1991-15 | 1992-17 | 1993-19 | 1994-23 | 1995-24 | 1996-23 |
| 1997-24 | 1998-24 | 1999-24 | 2000-25 | 2001-24 | 2002-24 |
| 2003-24 | 2004-23 | 2005-25 | 2006-26 | 2007-26 | 2008-25 |
| 2009-25 | 2010-25 | 2011-24 | 2012-26 | 2013-25 | 2014-24 |

The section has consistently been at the 24 club mark, or above, for the past 20 years as the above figures indicate and its present size is 24 clubs. A fine tribute to those pioneering gentlemen back in1983 and 1984.

A full programme of league and cup games on every weekend of the season provides a stepping stone into senior cricket for juniors, a more relaxed and less competitive platform for senior players and an opportunity to play for those who, for whatever reason, cannot play on Saturdays.

The awarding of batting and bowling points in addition to match points ensures interest in games is maintained even when the result is no longer in doubt and this encourages responsible endeavour in players and teams. This approach was pioneered in the Sunday Section long before being taken up by the Halifax Cricket League. This section of the League has a history of being the trial run for a number of rules that then became a rule in the Saturday League.

In 2014 the section will move to a 40 over format and a slightly earlier start time of 1.30pm in a bid to increase its attractiveness to school age players and their parents. This is in response to some of the findings in the first player's survey conducted by the ECB and YCB in 2013.

*Written by Gordon Akroyd and David Normanton*

TO BE DISCUSSED

Mr. Roy Smith,
President,
Halifax Cricket League.                    25th August, 1983.

Dear Roy,

      I refer to our recent conversation, and your request
to put in letter form the proposition to form a further division
for the third teams of the Halifax League teams to compete in,
instead of the Halifax Amateur League as at present.

      The foremost benefit would be to young players in the
fourteen and fifteen age bracket in being able to play on the
better prepared wickets of the Halifax League clubs, rather than
at places such as Roils Head where often it is positively
dangerous, and not fit for a young boy to take part.

      The only objection I can foresee at this time is the
unavailability of grounds, but I am sure this could be overcome
by some minor changes in the league fixtures. For example, only
one week break in July, instead of the present two weeks, would
give two further match dates; and there are two Bank Holidays
when there are no fixtures, namely, May Day and August, which
would give two more.

      If these measures did not produce enough extra match
dates, the Division could be split into smaller sections as at
present in junior cricket. There are probably other ideas that
Halifax League members would like to put foreward as well.

      I sincerely hope that this letter could be discussed
at your next meeting, and I look foreward to hearing from you.

          Yours very sincerely,

John M. Fraine

(Barkisland Third Team Captain)

# Sunday Section Officials

## PRESIDENTS

| | |
|---|---|
| 1985 - 1987 | R. SMITH |
| 1988 - 2003 | T. WYNNE |
| 2004 - | D. NORMANTON |

## CHAIRMEN

| | |
|---|---|
| 1985 | J. FRAINE |
| 1986 - 1988 | J. STANGER |
| 1989 - 2001 | R. KINNEAR |
| 2002 - 2005 | P. COLGAN |
| 2006 - | J. SUNDERLAND |

## SECRETARIES

| | |
|---|---|
| 1985 | J. STANGER |
| 1986 - 1997 | B. HAGUES |
| 1998 - 1999 | T. ATKINSON |
| 2000 - 2005 | N. MYERS |
| 2006 - 2012 | M. REPPION |
| 2013 - | G. M. AKROYD |

## TREASURERS

| | |
|---|---|
| 1985 - 1988 | R. KINNEAR |
| 1989 - 2001 | P. COLGAN |
| 2002 - 2012 and 2014 - | G. M. AKROYD |
| 2013 | M. REPPION |

## FIXTURE SECRETARIES

| | |
|---|---|
| 1988 - 2012 | N. MYERS |
| 2013 - | S. FINCH |

## ASSISTANT FIXTURE SECRETARIES

| | |
|---|---|
| 2012 | S. FINCH |
| 2013 - | N. MYERS |

# Sunday Section Honours

### LEAGUE CHAMPIONS

| | |
|---|---|
| 1985 | ILLINGWORTH |
| 1986 | OLD CROSSLEYANS |
| 1987 | HALIFAX |
| 1988 | HALIFAX |
| 1989 | BARKISLAND |
| 1990 | TODMORDEN |
| 1991 | UNION CROFT |
| 1992 | BLACKLEY |
| 1993 | BOOTH |
| 1994 | SOWERBY BRIDGE CHURCH INSTITUTE |

### SECTION A CHAMPIONS     SECTION B CHAMPIONS

| | SECTION A CHAMPIONS | SECTION B CHAMPIONS |
|---|---|---|
| 1995 | NORTHOWRAM | NORDEN |
| 1996 | BLACKLEY | HALIFAX |
| 1997 | NORTHOWRAM HEDGE TOP | NORDEN |
| 1998 | BOOTH | BLACKLEY |
| 1999 | TRIANGLE | OUTLANE |
| 2000 | NORDEN | BLACKLEY |
| 2001 | SOUTHOWRAM | SOWERBY BRIDGE |

### DIVISION 1 CHAMPIONS    DIVISION 2 CHAMPIONS    DIVISION 3 CHAMPIONS

| | DIVISION 1 CHAMPIONS | DIVISION 2 CHAMPIONS | DIVISION 3 CHAMPIONS |
|---|---|---|---|
| 2002 | TRIANGLE | LIGHTCLIFFE | BOOTH |
| 2003 | TRIANGLE | NORTHOWRAM HEDGE TOP | COPLEY |
| 2004 | SOWERBY BRIDGE | COPLEY | SOWERBY BRIDGE C.I. |
| 2005 | NORTHOWRAM HEDGE TOP | BOOTH | WARLEY |
| 2006 | TRIANGLE | NORDEN | **A** SOUTHOWRAM (play-off winners) **B** ELLAND |
| 2007 | NORTHOWRAM HEDGE TOP | ILLINGWORTH | **A** AUGUSTINIANS (play-off winners) **B** QUEENSBURY |
| 2008 | ILLINGWORTH | LIGHTCLIFFE | SOWERBY ST PETER'S |
| 2009 | NORDEN | RASTRICK | SOWERBY BRIDGE C. I. |
| 2010 | NORDEN | SOUTHOWRAM | NORTHOWRAM FIELDS |
| 2011 | BLACKLEY | AUGUSTINIANS | ELLAND |
| 2012 | AUGUSTINIANS | SOWERBY BRIDGE C.I. | OLD CROSSLEYANS |
| 2013 | LIGHTCLIFFE | ILLINGWORTH | SOWERBY BRIDGE |

## FRAINE/KENWORTHY TROPHY WINNERS

| | |
|---|---|
| 1989 | SOWERBY BRIDGE CHURCH INSTITUTE and STONES |
| 1990 | BLACKLEY |
| 1991 | BLACKLEY |
| 1992 | BOOTH and HALIFAX |
| 1993 | STONES |
| 1994 | BOOTH |
| 1995 | BLACKLEY |
| 1996 | NORDEN |
| 1997 | BOOTH |
| 1998 | SOWERBY BRIDGE |
| 1999 | SOUTHOWRAM |
| 2000 | BARKISLAND and RASTRICK |
| 2001 | TRIANGLE |
| 2002 | BARKISLAND |
| 2003 | BARKISLAND |
| 2004 | BLACKLEY |
| 2005 | LIGHTCLIFFE |
| 2006 | ELLAND |
| 2007 | COPLEY and SOWERBY ST PETER'S |
| 2008 | BLACKLEY |
| 2009 | KING CROSS |
| 2010 | MYTHOLMROYD |
| 2011 | ILLINGWORTH |
| 2012 | COPLEY |
| 2013 | THORNTON |

# Aspects of the League in pictures

**HALIFAX CRICKET LEAGUE**

**Official Handbook**

**Rules, Fixtures and Umpires**

**Season 1952**

TRINITY INSURANCE

# Halifax Cricket League

Trinity Insurance
Independent Insurance Advisers

MEMBERS OF THE YORKSHIRE CRICKET ASSOCIATION

President: D. NORMANTON , 98 Prospect Avenue, Pye Nest, Halifax HX2 7HP. Tel 01422 346371
Chairman: B. TENNYSON, 29, Greenacres, Shelf HX3 7HP. Tel 01422 346371
Hon. Secretary: LEYLAND SMITH, 16 St. Albans Avenue, Skircoat Green, Halifax HX3 7QT. Tel. 01422 675020
Assistant Secretary: NEIL MYERS, 31A Ford, Ambler Thorn, Queensbury, Halifax HX3 0LZ. Tel. 01422 365427
Hon. Treasurer: R. A. AIREY, 2, Wentworth Court Rastrick, Bradford BD13 2BJ Tel. 01274 882971
Hon. Fixture Secretary: M.J. SHEPPARD, "Roseneath", Stainland Road, Barkisland, Halifax HX4 0AG Tel. 01422 372404

**LEAGUE MEETING AGENDA**
**TUESDAY OCTOBER 5TH 2004**

1. Roll Call

2. Minutes of previous meeting

3. Correspondence

4. Treasurer's Report

5. Junior League Report

6. Umpires Report

7. Sunday League Report

8. Fixture Secretary's Report

9. The Press

10. Five-a-side Competition

11. Child Protection Issues

12. Annual Dinner

13. AGM

14. Heritage Project News and Update

15. Any other business

16. Date and time of next meeting

**HALIFAX CRICKET LEAGUE**
**LEAGUE MEETING MINUTES**
**TUESDAY 4TH MAY AT PELLON**

Members stood in silence to remember Arthur Smith, treasurer of Queensbury C.C. and a former stalwart of Hughes Green C.C. who had died recently.

Peter Davies, our League Historian spoke about the new grant for researching Cricket Clubs in Calderdale and Kirklees. He is sending letters to all clubs asking for support in allowing grounds to be mapped and signage to be arranged where clubs would like this service. He is very interested in clubs making available records, minute books etc., perhaps to be stored in the Library Archive Department. He will keep us updated at future meetings on this exciting project.

**1. Roll Call**

Apologies from Treasurer. Outlane absent. Agreed fined as per rule.

**2. Minutes of Previous Meeting** Accepted as a correct record.

**3. Correspondence**

- Umpires report. Bradshaw 2nds 9 men first Game. Mr Bell explained that a first teamer was injured during the game warm-up and a second teamer had to take his place. He apologised and assured the meeting that this would not happen again. It was agreed Bradshaw be fined as per rule
- Umpires Report. Greetland 2nds 8 men in Crossley Shield Game. Mr Forester said that due to the double header on a Bank Holiday weekend Greetland could not raise two teams. It was agreed Greetland be fined as per rule.
- Letter from Shelf saying that they have received permission from the Bradford Central League to apply for admission to our League for season 2005.
- Executive asked that the first six games for Mytholmroyd should have League or Umpires Association standing to monitor behaviour as agreed last year.
- Annual Dinner. Martin Gold comedian and Kevin Sharp have been booked.
- League Web Site. Steven Beverley with assistance from Gary Rodger have the site up and running with fixtures results and tables. Thanks to Keith Walker for his assistance. Hopefully Handbook details will be added. Please visit the site

**4. Treasurer's Report**

Cash in bank accounts £1631.14 and £2092.42 cash in hand £32.85. Cash in Benevolent Fund £1723.05. Invoices for club contributions to new trophies for the Conferences were issued to each representative

## HALIFAX CRICKET LEAGUE INDIVIDUAL PRIZE WINNERS SEASON 2004

|  |  |  |  | |  |  |
|---|---|---|---|---|---|---|
| Premier Division | Batting: | W. Ali | BOOTH | | RUNS | 1027 |
| | | | | | AVERAGE | 64.08 |
| | Bowling: | C. Greenwood | SOWERBY | | WKTS | 36 |
| | | | | | AVERAGE | 15.64 |
| | | | | | VICTIMS | 33 |
| | Wicketkeeping: | S. Priestley | COPLEY | | | |
| | Fielding | M. Shanks | THORNTON | | MARKS | 8 |
| Terry Wynne Conference | Batting: | G. Ahmed | GREETLAND | | RUNS | 486 |
| | | | | | AVERAGE | 40.50 |
| | Bowling: | M. Britton | GREETLAND | | WKTS | 63 |
| | | | | | AVERAGE | 10.54 |
| | | | | | VICTIMS | 23 |
| | Wicketkeeping: | S. Humphreys | OXENHOPE | | | |
| | | | | | MARKS | 7.5 |
| | Fielding | H. Singh | AUGUSTINIANS | | | |
| Roy Smith Conference | Batting: | I. Dobson | BLACKLEY | | RUNS | 704 |
| | | | | | AVERAGE | 47.00 |
| | Bowling: | S. White | OLD CROSSLEYANS | | WKTS | 49 |
| | | | | | AVERAGE | 12.71 |
| | | | | | VICTIMS | 19 |
| | Wicketkeeping: | J. Sykes | OLD CROSSLEYANS | | | |
| | Fielding | A. Greenwood | OLD TOWN | | MARKS | 7 |
| Premier Second | Batting: | J. Bullick | SOWERBY BRIDGE | | RUNS | 679 |
| | | | | | AVERAGE | 75.00 |
| | Bowling: | G. Grimley | SOWERBY | | WKTS | 38 |
| | | | | | AVERAGE | 11.08 |
| | | | | | VICTIMS | 16 |
| | Wicketkeeping: | J. Travis | SOWERBY | | | |
| | Fielding | J. Cartidge | BOOTH | | MARKS | 5.5 |
| Terry Wynne Conference Seconds | Batting: | P. Butterfield | THORNTON | | RUNS | 436 |
| | | | | | AVERAGE | 54.50 |
| | Bowling: | G. Lloyd | DENHOLME CLOUGH | | WKTS | 25 |
| | | | | | AVERAGE | 8.60 |
| | | | | | VICTIMS | 21 |
| | Wicketkeeping: | G. Pidgeon | GREETLAND | | | |
| | Fielding | J. Illingworth | QUEENSBURY | | MARKS | 5.5 |
| Roy Smith Conference Seconds | Batting: | A. Ingham | BRADSHAW | | RUNS | 557 |
| | | | | | AVERAGE | 69.63 |
| | Bowling: | A. Ingham | BRADSHAW | | WKTS | 38 |
| | | | | | AVERAGE | 7.82 |
| | | | | | VICTIMS | 16 |
| | Wicketkeeping: | B. Whitenead | BRIDGEHOLME | | | |
| | Fielding | J. Baxter | BLACKLEY | | MARKS | 7 |

### Sunday Section

|  |  |  |  | |  |  |
|---|---|---|---|---|---|---|
| Division 1 | Batting: | N. Twemlow | NORTHOWRAM | | RUNS | 445 |
| | | | | | AVERAGE | 63.75 |
| | Bowling: | M. Utley | TRIANGLE | | WKTS | 29 |
| | | | | | AVERAGE | 10.52 |
| | | | | | VICTIMS | 20 |
| | Wicketkeeping: | A. Raho | TRIANGLE | | | |
| | Fielding | J. Cavalier | TRIANGLE | | MARKS | 5 |
| Division 2 | Batting: | J. Shaw | LIGHTCLIFFE | | RUNS | 323 |
| | | | | | AVERAGE | 35.88 |
| | Bowling: | J. Harold | AUGUSTINIANS | | WKTS | 24 |
| | | | | | AVERAGE | 7.88 |
| | | | | | VICTIMS | 17 |
| | Wicketkeeping: | M. Barnett | BOOTH | | | |
| | Fielding | L. Thomas | BOOTH | | MARKS | 3.5 |
| Division 3 | Batting: | B. Hoyle | SOWERBY | | RUNS | 383 |
| | | | | | AVERAGE | 47.87 |
| | Bowling: | K. Doherty | ILLINGWORTH | | WKTS | 27 |
| | | | | | AVERAGE | 7.45 |
| | | | | | VICTIMS | 14 |
| | Wicketkeeping: | D. Patchett | ILLINGWORTH | | | |
| | Fielding | B. Hoyle | SOWERBY | | MARKS | 4 |

TRINITY INSURANCE
HALIFAX CRICKET LEAGUE
President: D. NORMANTON, Esq.

*Annual Dinner and*
*Prize Presentation*

ON FRIDAY 26th NOVEMBER 2004
AT ELLAND CRICKET CLUB

The President and Officers at the League extend a warm welcome to our Honoured Guests and all Friends of the League who have contributed to the success of last year.

Trinity Insurance

# HALIFAX CRICKET LEAGUE

President - D. Normanton

*Present*

# The Parish Cup Final

*Sponsored by*

**Briggs Priestley Limited**

At Copley C.C. on Sunday, August 1st, 2004
Wickets Pitched at 1.30pm

## *Copley C.C.* *v Warley C.C.*

Umpires
Mrs. E. Sykes, L. Forrester
Reserve - R. Wilkinson

---

**HALIFAX CRICKET LEAGUE 2001**
**Final League Tables**

**Section A**

| Team | P | W10 | W4 | Draw | L | Bonus | Total |
|---|---|---|---|---|---|---|---|
| Copley | 22 | 14 | 3 | 3* | 2 | 25 | 181 |
| Triangle | 22 | 12 | 3 | 5* | 2 | 31 | 169 |
| Warley | 22 | 7 | 7 | 4* | 4 | 51 | 154 |
| Booth | 22 | 9 | 4 | 2 | 7 | 44 | 152 |
| Sowerby Bridge | 22 | 6 | 6 | 2 | 8 | 48 | 134 |
| Northowram | 22 | 4 | 7 | 4 | 7 | 59 | 131 |
| Sowerby | 22 | 6 | 4 | 1 | 11 | 48 | 125 |
| Outlane | 22 | 6 | 0 | 2 | 14 | 45 | 107 |
| Bradshaw | 22 | 3 | 2 | 8* | 9 | 56 | 103 |
| SBCI | 22 | 2 | 5 | 4 | 11 | 58 | 102 |
| Southowram | 22 | 2 | 4 | 4 | 12 | 57 | 97 |
| Myth. Meths. | 22 | 4 | 0 | 1 | 17 | 41 | 82 |

**Section B**

| Team | P | W10 | W4 | Draw | L | Bonus | Total |
|---|---|---|---|---|---|---|---|
| Blackley | 22 | 9 | 7 | 4 | 2 | 45 | 167 |
| Augustinians | 22 | 10 | 3 | 6 | 3 | 36 | 154 |
| Mytholmroyd | 22 | 8 | 6 | 4 | 4 | 41 | 149 |
| Luddenden Foot | 22 | 7 | 5 | 2 | 8 | 50 | 142 |
| Stainland | 22 | 8 | 4 | 5 | 5 | 39 | 140 |
| Old. Crocs | 22 | 8 | 3 | 7 | 4 | 36 | 135 |
| Old Town | 22 | 5 | 5 | 7 | 5 | 47 | 124 |
| Bridgeholme | 22 | 6 | 1 | 3 | 12 | 45 | 112 |
| Greetland | 22 | 5 | 1 | 2 | 14 | 52 | 108 |
| Queensbury | 22 | 6 | 1 | 1 | 11 | 34 | 102 |
| S. Nook O. B. | 22 | 4 | 1 | 4 | 13 | 40 | 88 |
| Stones | 22 | 3 | 1 | 4 | 14 | 50 | 88 |

\* Inc. Tie

18

---

**HALIFAX CRICKET LEAGUE 2001**
**Final League Tables**

**Section C**

| Team | P | W10 | W4 | Draw | L | Bonus | Total |
|---|---|---|---|---|---|---|---|
| Triangle | 22 | 13 | 5 | 2 | 2 | 29 | 181 |
| Northowram | 22 | 8 | 2 | 4 | 8 | 48 | 140 |
| Warley | 22 | 8 | 4 | 3 | 7 | 38 | 137 |
| Sowerby Bridge | 22 | 7 | 5 | 4 | 6 | 41 | 135 |
| Copley | 22 | 5 | 7 | 2 | 8 | 53 | 133 |
| Southowram | 22 | 7 | 2 | 5 | 8 | 37 | 120 |
| Stainland | 22 | 5 | 4 | 2 | 11 | 52 | 120 |
| Booth | 22 | 8 | 0 | 2 | 12 | 35 | 117 |
| Sowerby | 22 | 6 | 3 | 7 | 6 | 37 | 116 |
| Outlane | 22 | 6 | 3 | 4 | 9 | 38 | 114 |
| Old Town | 22 | 4 | 3 | 6 | 9 | 42 | 100 |
| Bradshaw | 22 | 3 | 1 | 5 | 13 | 29 | 68 |

**Section D**

| Team | P | W10 | W4 | Draw | L | Bonus | Total |
|---|---|---|---|---|---|---|---|
| Augustinians | 22 | 16 | 2 | 2 | 2 | 12 | 182 |
| Old Crocs | 22 | 15 | 1 | 1 | 5 | 18 | 173 |
| Blackley | 22 | 12 | 4 | 2 | 4 | 34 | 172 |
| S.B.C.I. | 22 | 11 | 4 | 2 | 5 | 31 | 161 |
| Greetland | 22 | 9 | 1 | 2 | 10 | 33 | 129 |
| Mytholmroyd | 22 | 4 | 7 | 2 | 9 | 51 | 121 |
| Bridgeholme | 22 | 6 | 2 | 4 | 10 | 42 | 114 |
| Queensbury | 22 | 6 | 1 | 3 | 12 | 36 | 103 |
| Luddenden Foot | 22 | 7 | 0 | 2 | 13 | 30 | 102 |
| Stones | 22 | 4 | 3 | 5* | 10 | 38 | 96 |
| S.Nook O.B. | 22 | 3 | 1 | 3* | 15 | 38 | 76 |
| Myth. Meths | 22 | 2 | 2 | 4 | 14 | 39 | 71 |

\* Inc. Tie

19

# Personal Recollections & Reminiscences

## BLACKLEY CRICKET CLUB

Blackley in the late 1950's was a sleepy little village but its cricket club was a hive of activity. I was introduced to it via the Ladies Tuesday Night Whist Drives organised by Mrs. Alice Dyson for over fifty years. These were held in the wooden tearoom, heated by an iron pot-bellied stove fed with coal, which members brought in little bags. Later this was replaced by overhead electric heaters which gave hot heads and cold feet. Everyone contributed towards the supper. It was a cheerful room with green and white curtains and tablecloths.

Tuesday evenings were the time to catch up with the local gossip, organise future events and check the tea rota. Few ladies worked in those days resulting in you only having to do your share on the tea rota two or three times. Cricket teas consisted of tea cakes - provided locally by Hanson's Bakery and homemade cakes and buns.

During the day the retired men got from under their wives' feet to play cards, dominoes, drink tea and read the Courier. There was always something happening.

Various moneymaking events were planned each year by the club. Fashion, make-up, talks and Tupperware Parties were held. One memorable occasion was a ladies' dinner with a beautiful meal prepared by the men with surprise entertainment which turned out to be a male stripper!

Trips were organised. Whittle's Bakery, arriving home with sample packs of meat pies, bread and cakes. Greenall Whitley Brewery where, after a tour, we were treated to lunch, and, after waiting several years, the Leeds City Varieties entertained us, all decked out in our Victorian costumes. Our members at that show appeared on a picture on the cover of the Christmas record.

There was a Ladies Cricket Team who played against the men, who had to bowl left handed. Annual Whist Drives and Dances were held at the Civic Hall in West Vale with a real band. The Council allowed clubs to have cake stalls in the Elland Market once a year. Smaller events were held in the club, jumble sales, bring and buy, race nights, beetle drives and one year an Autumn Fair with traditional games, roll a penny, tombola, bran tub, mini matches and a beer tent.

During the winter months waste paper was collected and stored in the old tea rooms which were used as the men's changing rooms. Waggons would be loaded via a human chain.

In 1970, the M62 came along slicing through the village taking in its wake houses, a chapel, an inn and part of the cricket field.

In 1976 the club was given a new piece of land upon which to build a new clubhouse. The first attempt was a pre-cast structure which lasted a week before a gale ripped the roof off and demolished it. It was replaced by the brick built pavilion which is now our pride and joy. Money had to be raised and the sale of alcohol was debated with opposition from older members but we moved with the times.

Players and members are now spread over a larger area and with the possibility of new houses on the former brickworks the future looks bright.

New faces, new ideas, but still the happy family club of the 50's.

*Article by Mabel Pighills aged 80(ish)*
*Lifetime resident of Blackley and Life Member of Blackley CC*

# BOOTH CRICKET CLUB

### Valley's Luscious Greenery

High above Luddenden and Luddendenfoot, and just down the road from Wainstalls and Mount Tabor, lies Booth, known primarily for cotton and silk and its handsome Congregational chapel (built in 1869 and likened by one architectural historian to a 'miniature cathedral').

Writer James Birdsall comments: 'Scarcely a village, but a twin row of old terraced weavers' cottages, Booth clings on to the flank of a ravine in the hills above the Calder Valley.'

The cricket ground, set amid luscious greenery, is only a matter of yards from the bus terminus and the narrow, winding road that is Dean House Lane.

If there was an award for well-kept cricket grounds, just as there is one for well-kept railway stations, Booth would have to be in with a shout.

### Sturdy Sightscreens

The playing area resembles a large, slightly sloping putting green, and the tall emerald green trees that surround the venue are handsome.

The sightscreens are sturdy and wheeled, and there's a lovely curved wall on the far side of the ground, on top of which hardy supporters congregate - even when it's raining.

There's also a public bridleway running nearby.

### Groundless Early Years

In the early years of their existence, Booth were ground-less and tended to play in farmers' fields that were also inhabited by cows. (A photo of the Congregational church taken in 1911 shows a game of cricket being played in a hillside field beyond the village).

However, in 1946 permission was granted to construct a permanent headquarters at Broadfold. Building work took place in 1947, which meant that all the club's 'home' games during that season had to be played away.

### Building Work

The new ground was opened on 24 April 1948.
In 1950 work was carried out to reduce the slope, and in 1972 builders started on the pavilion. Thirty years on, the kitchen is always busy, the walls are awash with team photos - from 1912, 1948, 1949, 1952, 1958 and later - and a blue club flag flatters from the building's roof.

### Clocks and Boxes

There were further developments in the 1980s: the pavilion was extended, a new car park was built, and showers were installed.

Today, there's a BBQ by the changing rooms, pretty flowers in the hanging baskets, and cut-price teas available for kids on matchdays.

The new scorebox clock is dedicated to the memory of Rod Warhurst, a long-serving club member.

Over the years Booth have struck up a fierce but friendly local rivalry with Luddendenfoot (primarily) and Mytholmroyd.

### Small and Attractive

Booth may be a small village, with only a few rows of terraces, but its cricket ground is definitely worth a visit.

# BRADSHAW CRICKET CLUB

Bradshaw - in the far north-western corner of Calderdale - is one of the highest parts of Halifax, with the ground standing 919 feet above sea level. Queensbury, just the other side of the local government boundary, lies approximately 1,100 feet above sea level.

Bradshaw has had a cricket team since 1923. In the early days, the club played in the Halifax Association, but in 1954 it joined the Halifax League; the glory days came in the 1990s when the 1st XI won the League twice (1992 and 1997) and the Parish Cup once (1991).

The image of a white castle dominates their club crest - due recognition of the fact that White Castle Breweries owned the Bradshaw Lane ground in yesteryear.

The club's ground is visible from Bradshaw Lane - situated just behind houses, tennis courts and the local bowling green. Legend has it that only one batsman in 80 years has managed to clear the boundary, and the farmer's field that lies beyond it, and deposited the ball onto the bowling green.

The ground lies adjacent to the Bradshaw Tavern. Indeed, visitors to the pub can watch the action from inside the bar, and drinkers who wander out into the beer garden can see the game at even closer quarters.

In the early 1990s, the pub actually became famous. Trans World Sport, an international television company, were looking for a venue for the Knur and Spell World Championships (K & S is an early, antiquated form of golf). The TV people liked the look of the pub, and the ground, and brought the event to Bradshaw - in their view, an ideal and hugely picturesque venue.

From the A647, the Bradshaw Lane ground looks like it is located on a steep slope; when you are actually at the ground, you don't notice the pronounced fall down from the pavilion to the far boundary, but it is a gentle slope, and nothing more. It's a windy spot, but on a sunny day, when the shadow of the pavilion stretches out onto the outfield, it's also a very pleasant spot.

Club spokesman Mick Turner says that opposition players like visiting Bradshaw: 'They appreciate the facilities, but they're always a little wary about the weather. If it's not a sunny day, they know it will be pretty chilly!'

Plans were under discussion in 1959 for a pavilion to be built and fencing would also be altered. At a meeting it was decided that the pavilion could not cost more than the £273 that was quoted by the National Playing Fields Association. The new pavilion was officially opened on 29 May 1960.

A 15-mile walk was arranged in order to raise money for the club's memorial gates. In September 1968 they were officially opened, a short service was conducted by the Vicar of Bradshaw, and a cricket match followed. Bradshaw celebrated their 50th birthday in 1973 by organising a dinner at the Saxon Hotel which was attended by many ex-players.

In 1978 a Mr T. Corbett asked the club if six sheep could graze on the outfield. The club committee immediately agreed – realising that this was a means of ensuring the grass was kept short!

Today Bradshaw is a successful club with a beautiful ground – the highest in Calderdale.

## BRIDGEHOLME CRICKET CLUB

Preparation of the Station House ground had been underway since the summer of 1952. Drainage, levelling and the laying of the square had been the priorities.

The first match, against Hebden Bridge Salem in the first division of the Hebden Bridge and District League, was scheduled for 9 May 1953 but the ground was not quite ready and the game was switched to Salem Field.

Bridgeholme captain John Martin hit 125 of his side's 222 all out that afternoon, the first century by a Bridgeholme batsman and the first time the team had scored 200.

The ground was opened ten days later on the evening of Tuesday 19 May, just a fortnight before the coronation of Queen Elizabeth II.

The 1st XI beat Heptonstall Slack seconds by eight wickets in the Hebden Bridge League's 20 overs-a-side knockout cup, Jack Kaye taking 7 for 20 with his off-spinners as the visitors were all out for 40.

The first League match on the ground was played the following Saturday when the 2nd XI beat Old Town seconds by 54 runs.

The first eleven made their home League debut on 30 May and suffered one of only three defeats that season, replying to Birchcliffe's 174 with 99 all out.

With the construction of the new pavilion has come the opportunity to provide post-match hospitality, thereby earning much needed funds, at the ground.

It is a condition of the Lottery grant which funded the building that it is used by the community, and local groups and private individuals are taking advantage of Eastwood's first community building for decades.

The last of the town's many all-amateur clubs, Bridgeholme is somewhat dwarfed by the town's other two clubs, Todmorden and Walsden.

Bridgeholme's Keith Hudson explains the pros and cons of the local competition: 'If we develop a player who becomes particularly good, we're going to lose them, probably as an amateur to Todmorden or Walsden, although some have been offered money to play.

'On the other hand, we are still developing our youth set-up and have been grateful to acquire players from the Todmorden and Walsden junior teams who probably aren't going to make the first team there, or who just prefer our set up.

'We know our place but we're a friendly club. We may not be the best cricketers around, but we can play the game as sportingly as anyone else. Some clubs find it strange when we applaud the opposition, but we are proud to play the game that way.

## CLAYTON CRICKET CLUB

Clayton is located about 220 metres above sea level at the south end of a relatively flat ridge of land on the south side of Clayton Beck Valley. The valley drops steeply below this shoulder of land and rises steeply to the south, south-east and south-west. The soil is, unsurprisingly, mainly of a clay in character but there are deposits of sandstone and gritstone.

The village is three miles from Bradford city centre, with the village of Thornton located on the other side of the valley and the village of Queensbury further up the hill that Clayton is situated on. Clayton Beck runs though the bottom of the valley below Clayton and tributaries for this stream, including Bull Grieve Beck, run through the village.

The centre of the village was designated as a conservation area in 1977. The main street of the village – Clayton Lane – which runs alongside the park, includes several traditional pubs, a popular crawl route for many residents. The now-defunct Clayton Tide newspaper described the central role of the pubs in Clayton village life in a 15 August 1861 account of a visit to the village by Pablo Fanque, the popular Victorian circus owner who The Beatles later immortalised in the song Being for the Benefit of Mr. Kite! The Clayton Tide reported, "On Sunday, a great number of persons visited the village, but ignoring the "Teetotal Lectures" which were given at Town Bottom, the public houses were well attended. Mr Pablo Fanque, always welcome on such occasions, was present and a damsel in his company, who emulated Blondin's feats, drew a large crowd."

Clayton boasts several shops, churches, and a nearby golf club and country park at Thornton View with views of the city of Bradford and the village of Thornton across the valley.

Clayton has amateur sports teams in football, rugby, cricket and bowls. Clayton Cricket Club was founded in 1951, and moved to the Halifax Cricket League in 2007. They have two senior Teams (1st & 2nd Team) while the junior set up has 3 teams this season in the Halifax Junior Cricket League, at Under 11's, Under 13's & Under 17's ages.

The clubs honours in the Halifax League include winning the Terry Wynne 2nd Division 1st Team Championship in 2009 and the Terry Wynne 2nd Division 2nd team Championship in 2008.

At the Junior level, they have won their 'area' League titles at Under 17 level (2012), Under 13 level (2012 & 2013), Under 11 level (2013) and the Under 9's Cricket Festival in 2013. Clearly junior cricket is thriving in Clayton.

The Cricket Club has recently completed building a new pavilion to bring them up to the 21st Century with modern facilities. The building work has been completed by Paul Cornforth, the ex Clayton Rugby League player. The new club house was officially opened by the Deputy Lord Mayor, Cllr Mike Gibbons on Sunday 8 July 2012. Local residents, businesses and club members have worked together to help replace the old club house, helped by funding from Bradford Council and Clayton Parish Council.

**Little known facts**

Clayton is the birthplace and was the home of Albert Pierrepoint, Great Britain's last state executioner. He held the position until 1956. His father Henry Albert Pierrepoint, born in Clayton in 1876, was also a state executioner.

Abe Waddington was also born in Clayton, on 4 February 1893. Abe was a bowler in the English cricket team of 1920-21.

## COPLEY CRICKET CLUB

*Past League President – Roy Smith, Copley Cricket Club*

Roy Smith was a driving force behind the Halifax Cricket League and the development of local cricket for nearly half a century and was League President from 1971 until 1988.

Roy died in 1997 having been a member of Copley Cricket Club for seventy years. As a player, Roy was a top quality wicketkeeper and aggressive opening batsman. He won the Copley fielding prize no less than ten times, a club record, and claimed the batting prize on seven occasions. He was Copley Cricket Club's Chairman from 1955 until 1965 and President between 1965 and 1997.

Roy's contribution to local cricket was immeasurable and his influence without question. During his leadership, the League began to establish itself in a Yorkshire context and Roy was well known in County circles. He was also responsible for establishing the Halifax Junior Cricket League. He was an inspirational character to many generations of local cricket players and supporters, during a life that was devoted to Copley Cricket Club, the development of local cricket and the Halifax Cricket League. In Halifax he was known as 'Mr Cricket'; in Yorkshire he was known as 'Mr Halifax'.

In 2012 Copley Cricket Club achieved national recognition for its new £585,000 pavilion development and for being awarded National Showcase status by the ECB under the NatWest CricketForce initiative, the largest community volunteering programme in UK sport.

The project to build a new pavilion and to widen the club's community focus had taken 7 years – since being made a Focus Club by the YCB in 2005 and achieving the Clubmark accreditation in the following year. The club's commitment to develop its Junior Section and also to re-invest the proceeds of the sale of a small strip of land to a neighbouring housing development, were both major factors in the launch of the project. After many years of fundraising and applying for grants, the project started to attract local support and funding from outside of the area. The key to the project's success has ultimately been the financial support that has been received from the ECB, but the club also received other grants from SITA Trust, Awards for All and Calderdale

Council. The club engaged the local community and attracted many additional local sponsors and as a consequence 2012 has been an extremely busy and rewarding year for Copley Cricket Club. 2012 has also seen the formation of South Halifax Girls, which is the first girl's cricket team in Calderdale, and attracts players who are able to remain members of other Halifax League Clubs.

The publicity has also promoted the Halifax Cricket League at a national level with a range of articles and photographs appearing in national newspapers, websites and cricket magazines such as The Cricketer. The programme for the England / South Africa test match at Headingley also featured a double page feature on the new pavilion project and Copley's NatWest CricketForce achievements. In August 2012, Copley Cricket Club was awarded an OSCA by the YCB at its annual awards ceremony at Headingley for its contribution to NatWest CricketForce.

**The timeline for Copley's NatWest CricketForce Showcase year has been as follows:**

August 2011 – NWCF National Showcase Family Fun Day – supported by Michael Vaughan, Tim Bresnan, Jenny Gunn and Katherine Brunt;

September 2011 – appointment of building contractor and launch of additional fundraising and sponsorship initiatives;

October 2011 – demolition of old pavilion and preparation of site for building;

November 2011 – commencement of building work;

December 2011 – erection of steel frame;

January 2012 – Public Meeting to promote NWCF and to engage the community in the project;

January 2012 – launch of South Halifax Girls and creation of partnership with Calderdale College;

February 2012 – Continued fundraising and "door knocking" to support NWCF;

February 2012 – erection of roof;

March 2012 – 24 hour continuous "Bike – a – thon" fundraising event;

April 2012 – NWCF Showcase Day – supported by Mike Gatting, Neil Fairbrother and 250 members and community supporters;

May 2012 – Volunteers continue to support the "finishing aspects" of the project – a race against time and a challenging start to the new season. Opening of changing rooms and the new bar;

May 2012 – first fixture for South Halifax Girls;

May 2012 – the staging of the first "major game" – Yorkshire X1 (captained by Richard Pyrah) narrowly beat a Halifax Cricket League Presidents X1;

June 2012 – The floods! Copley Cricket Club becomes a lake, being submerged under two feet of floodwater for several weeks – with floodwater causing considerable damage to the new pavilion;

July 2012 – No cricket played in the aftermath of the floods and the "finishing projects" have to be replaced by a "mopping up" exercise and repair work;

August 2012 – although playing conditions remain "under repair," cricket starts again after being flooded for 6 weeks;

August 2012 – Copley Cricket Club awarded an OSCA by the Yorkshire Cricket Board at their annual awards ceremony under the NWCF category and invited to attend the ECB's national awards day at Lords;

September 2012 – The Official Opening of the New Pavilion and the staging of West Yorkshire Girls Cricket Finals, featuring South Halifax Girls;

October 2012 – the new pavilion begins to be used for a wider variety of community activities.

As one can see, the last year has been a "roller coaster" ride for Copley Cricket Club and its members and community supporters, who have all worked continuously to achieve their new facilities. By its own admission, the Club now looks forward to a period of consolidation, to ensure that "normal service" can be resumed, and to re-focus on cricket development. Steve Archer the West Yorkshire Development Manager for the YCB deserves a special mention and Copley Cricket Club also wishes to thank the ECB and all their funding partners and supporters. The Club also wish to record their particular thanks to Dave Normanton and the Executive of the Halifax Cricket League who have been active supporters throughout the entire project and every aspect of what has been a very busy year.

## CULLINGWORTH CRICKET CLUB

Cullingworth are the 58th club to play in the Halifax Cricket League and put forward their reasons for wanting to leave the Mewies Solicitors Craven League at the Application League Meeting in March 2013 for acceptance to 2014 season.

The Roydwood Terrace club applied to join the Halifax Cricket League for the 2014 season, and club chairman Steve Welch was part of their presentation to the League Meeting at Pellon Social Club.

He said: "We don't think that the Craven League match the ambition that we have as a club. We also think that the cricket in the Halifax Cricket League will be better."

Cullingworth won the Craven League championship in 2007, 2008 and 2009, also lifting the Wynn Cup for first teams in 2005, 2007, 2008 and 2012.

Club Secretary Iain Wilson talked of ground improvements, saying: "In the last five years we have spent heavily on resurfacing the new car park, installing new toilets, a boiler and showers and refurbishing the bar and refreshment areas."

Welch also stressed the community aspect of the club and the willingness of players and administrators to help out.

He added: "The first team is very competitive but off the pitch we are very sociable.

"The second team hasn't always been as competitive but over the past four years we have started to mature and develop, and in the last two years we have introduced some of our juniors to senior cricket."

Phil Poole junior, joint coach of Cullingworth Cobras under-11s, said: "We are in our fifth season in the Upper Airedale Junior Cricket Association and have had an under-11 team in there for the past four years.

"We have teams at under-nines, 11s, 13s and 15s, and last year we had two 14 year-olds in the first team, five juniors representing Yorkshire and over ten lads in the League or Bradford Schools' junior sides."

We welcome them as the newest members and wish them well as we commence season 2014.

## DENHOLME CLOUGH CRICKET CLUB

Denholme Clough Cricket Club is a cricket club playing in the Halifax Cricket League.

We currently run two adult teams on a Saturday but as the club is steadily growing, we have plans for Sunday and Junior teams is the very new future.

The club has recently grown stronger not only in numbers but financially too. We have adopted an approach of inviting local businesses to share the chance to be involved through ground advertising possibilities and so, pull the community of Denholme and parts of Halifax together.

We have a young team with a few wise old heads which should see us well for the future. The foundations are strong and we can only prosper and hopefully soon be able to compete with the bigger clubs of the Halifax Cricket League.

Last year saw the end of one era and the beginning of another. We adopted a new committee, full of ideas, enthusiasm and eager to put the hard thinking that has taken place into practise. Small changes in securing larger local business to pay more attention to the new ethos of the club paid dividends enabling us carry out new projects to revamp the club. With volunteers and a lot of elbow grease, the newly developed score box and patio have revitalised the club, as well as passions and love for the game, after all we all play cricket for the love of the game.

The future of the club looks bright with the Denholme Velvet Mills hopefully soon giving way to redevelopment of town houses, bringing with it not only the ownership of the land to the cricket club and the security that it offers, but with it a new young community on our door step. The possibilities of a recreational area for them to feel proud of, spend time at and adding value to, can only be classed as progress. It is amazing that a mill that provided so much for the club in the beginning is still playing such a big role in the development, growth and prosperity of the club today over a 100 years on.

Much love from all at Denholme Clough.

*Mohammed Yousaf (Mo)*

# GREETLAND CRICKET CLUB

Greetland's headquarters, 'The Holme' on Saddleworth Road, plays host to cricket, bowling and pigeon-racing.

Perched high on the scoreboard side of the ground are half a dozen sizeable pigeon coops. Members of Stainland and District Homing Society use Greetland Cricket and Bowling Club (as it is formally known) as their base, and the pavilion notice board is full of race details and times. One local pigeon-fancier drives a vehicle with the number-plate: P1GON !

As you sit in the pavilion, you can actually see the pigeons looking out of their wire cages - a rare and possibly unique sight at a Calderdale cricket venue. Sometimes a Greetland cricket fixture coincides with a race day, so on such occasions there are two attractions for the price of one. 'Holme' is an ancient Scandinavian word denoting 'a flat piece of ground near a river' - hence the name of Greetland's pleasant, well enclosed ground. The cricket club has never played anywhere else.

No-one quite knows when cricket was first played at the ground; the 1890's is the best bet, but a dust-ridden framed photo hidden away in the pavilion features five key personalities in the early history of the club - JW Sykes (1894), F Webster (1929), JJ Fielden (1911), N Saville (1931) and AL Richardson (1934). So the cricket club is at least 120 years old.

In the 1930's a local blanket manufacturer, John Horsfall's (based on Stainland Road), donated the ground to Greetland as a gift. The club was charged just a peppercorn rent - sixpence a year. During the early years of the twentieth century, Greetland had its fair share of colourful characters: for instance, Jack Hayes, who started at the club as a junior, and Percy Smith, the village cobbler and a man who emerged as one of the club's most important patrons.

It was Smith who also helped flood the bottom of the ground in winter so that locals could play ice hockey and go skating! There is also evidence to suggest that a Greetland Ladies team existed in the early part of the last century.

Greetland is located two and a half miles south of Halifax and a mile or so west of Elland. Indeed, in days gone by, it was part of a township called Elland-cum-Greetland.

The small village is home to three noteworthy buildings: Clay House, Sunny Bank and Toll-Bar House, from where, centuries ago, a turnpike official used to monitor all users of the main road that passed through Greetland. And a bit of modern-day trivia: the Calderdale Way, no less, begins in the village.

The village is only small, but until recently it boasted two cricket teams. In addition to Greetland CC there was Greetland Village CC, formed in the 1980s by three or four former Greetland CC players. Greetland Village were members of the Halifax Association and played at the Goldfields complex on Rochdale Road.

The Holme may have seen better days, but it still has its charm as a local league cricket venue: the now disused scorebox set back from the playing area, the trickling stream that runs nearby, the Black Beck, which eventually joins the Calder, not forgetting the quaint and slightly narrow mini-bridge that the scorers had to navigate to get to and from the scorebox.

Then there's the unusual white corrugated boundary board on the same side of the ground, and the huge, elaborate, almost spherical clock that sits in the backyard of Andy Thornton, architectural antiques merchant, whose premises back onto the cricket field on the opposite side. And for the record, none of the clock's faces tell the right time!

That a cricket ground is wedged between Rochdale Road and Saddleworth Road is not obvious to the first-time visitor. It is enclosed on one side by large buildings and on the other by a dense wooded area - and hidden from view behind the new Cooperative Supermarket - but it has been Greetland CC's home patch for more than a century. Today, some visiting players still reckon it's one of the flattest grounds in the area.

Club stalwart Betts says: 'Greetland were a top side in the 1950's and 1960's, but now things are different. When opposition sides come here, they're almost guaranteed the points! But the club has its own ground, which has got to be a blessing, and in people like Les Forrester and Harold Sykes, we have been blessed with wonderful, wholehearted servants in recent times.'

A plaque in the pavilion lounge pays tribute to another dedicated club man, 2nd XI captain John Redhead, who died tragically in 2001.

## JER LANE CRICKET CLUB

An open top bus parade was hailed a success as the club celebrated being Halifax League Premier Division Champions in 2013. This was the first time that a Halifax Cricket League Club had celebrated in this way.

Jer Lane's victory parade to celebrate their Foster's Halifax League triumphs of the summer of 2013 was a success.

The club's first team were Halifax Cricket League Champions and Parish Cup Winners with their second team chipping in by being Roy Smith 1st division Champions.

The Horton Bank Top club hired an open top bus and toured the area near their ground before heading off to Halifax and Sowerby Bridge.

"It was very successful - everyone loved it," said organiser Andrew Pinfield, who was an opening batsman for the year's Premier Division Champions and Parish Cup winners.

Andrew Pinfield reported that favourable weather had been "a godsend" and people had emerged from houses to watch the spectacle, some with banners of support. Pinfield also confirmed that a number of their players and supporters had partied at the club afterwards.

The Cricket Club had earlier in 2013 said farewell to club stalwart Karl Laban, who died suddenly aged 54 in May. Karl was a one-club man who started his career as a 14-year-old in the early 1970s and was identified as a promising pace bowler.

Former Jer Lane player Ken Gill said: "Karl worked very hard on his game and made himself into a good fast bowler." Long-serving club members Derek Wilson and Malcolm Nixon also praised Karl for his tireless involvement in the development of facilities at Jer Lane, which are now unrecognisable to when he first came to the club.

Known to many as a fierce competitor with a never-to-be beaten attitude, Karl was also held in high esteem by opposition teams and would always enjoy the social side of league cricket.

During Jer Lane's tenure in the Bradford Central League, Karl won league bowling prizes on a number of occasions.

Karl's legacy is continued through his sons Nathan, Jordan and Daniel, who all play in the current Jer Lane senior teams.

## LOW MOOR HOLY TRINITY CRICKET CLUB

The club was accepted into the Halifax Cricket League in 2007 and we have been made very welcome by David Normanton and all the officials of the League. We are very happy to be part of such a well organised League.

Congratulations on reaching your Centenary and best wishes for another 100 years.

Our proudest moment so far has been reaching the Parish Cup Final in 2012 where we lost to S.B.C.I. at Sowerby St Peter's.

We sprung a major upset when we knocked out Premier League table toppers Booth at the semi-final stage. Low Moor were bottom of Division One and we travelled as huge underdogs but left with a famous victory after outplaying our illustrious hosts throughout.

Our stand-in skipper Graham Scarborough won the toss and elected to field first, his team produced an outstanding bowling display to restrict the 2011 beaten finalists to 182, with our youngest players leading the way.

However we, very much the underdogs again, were defeated by 26 runs in the rain-interrupted final contest by SBCI, who thus won the first-team knockout climax for the second time in three years.

SBCI resumed on 153-5 after the contest had been interrupted by heavy rainfall on the original scheduled date and added 62 runs for the loss of three wickets in the final ten overs.

Our skipper Nick Wood and Mark Stokes picked up the wickets of experienced left-hander Craig Potts for 45 and Matthew Scholefield for four, who departed to a smart stumping by Carl Harrison.

We were without the services of Mark Mills on the resumption date and replied with 189, Carl Harrison hitting 58 and Stokes 40 but SBCI skipper Jamie Sykes took two wickets in two balls to turn the final their way and earn the man-of-the-match award.

We thoroughly enjoyed our time in the limelight and look forward to many more splendid occasions.

# LUDDENDENFOOT CRICKET CLUB

Luddendenfoot's ground, high up on the south bank of the River Calder, is surrounded by farmers' fields, winding valley roads, dry stone walls, enticing cottages and greenery unlimited. From the pavilion, the Calder Valley panorama is magnificent: to the west, Hebden Bridge and surrounds; to the east, Sowerby Bridge and satellite communities; and straight in front, the handsome north bank of the river, complete with gleaming-white wind turbines on the far horizon.

So, on account of its high, rural location, the ground has its appeal for opposition players. It is also viewed as a good wicket to bat on. One opposition batsman declared: 'I like coming here because it's a small venue and the boundaries are pretty short. But the other side of the coin is that there's a lot of bounce, so some bowlers can put up with the short boundaries because they know they'll always get a bit of life out of the pitch.'

The playing area is neatly marked out, the sightscreens are on rollers, and there are several rows of benches in front of the pavilion building. There is also a neat little stone path for incoming and outgoing batsmen to navigate.

The pavilion comprises changing rooms, tea area and lounge. As one waits for the barman, one can peruse the many and various team photos that line the top rim of the bar. And from the posters on display, it is clear that there is always a lot going on - even a 'Fun & Frolics' day (whatever that is exactly). One visiting spectator says: 'Great facilities for children and a friendly club - if just a little exposed!'

In the early days, there were two buildings at the ground: one hut housed changing rooms and scorers; the other, the tea room. Both, however, were destroyed by fire.

In the 1970s, the club erected a prefabricated building that, in the context of its era, was state-of-the- art. It was home to changing and tea-making facilities, but still lacked running water and electricity.

Then, in 1997, the club opened a new enlarged pavilion complex - basically, a new prefab added on to the old one. The club got showers, a new storeroom and a new tea room. For this project, the club gained financial support from the Foundation for Sport and the Arts.

To the right of the pavilion is a farmer's field with a pond, known locally as 'The Dam'. It is not a case of losing cricket balls in The Dam, but rather cricketers. After the last match of the season, or as the club celebrates a championship triumph or a famous cup victory, club members have been known to celebrate in soaking fashion.

There is a definite family atmosphere at High Lee Green: mums and dads in deckchairs or picnicking around the ground, teenagers on duty in the scorebox, and a cosy little playground for younger children just to the side of the pavilion. This area is cordoned off with high netting, so the kiddies are protected from any firmly hit sixes or fours.

But locals must beware ! A sign by the main entrance to the ground says unambiguously: PLEASE DO NOT ALLOW YOUR DOGS TO USE THIS FIELD AS A TOILET!

# MYTHOLMROYD CRICKET CLUB

*Photo is an image of Charlie Pugh and Bert Wilcock (Charlie on the left)*

Not to be confused with its less famous cousin from the south, Marylebone Cricket Club, the true M.C.C., Mytholmroyd Cricket Club was formed circa 1895 and cricket is recorded as being played at its present ground Ewood Holmes since this date, a most picturesque ground under the gaze of the imposing Scout Rocks in the Upper Calder Valley.

Halcyon days for the Halifax Cricket League founder member club being a dominant force within the Halifax Cricket League were during the 30's, 40's and 50's. It was during this very successful period that a remarkable and surely unique piece of cricketing history was made at Mytholmroyd.

In the season of 1948 Mytholmroyd were duly crowned Halifax League Champions under the captaincy of H (Goff) Ellis. This would largely have been due to the exploits of the opening bowling partnership of Charles (Charlie) Pugh and Herbert (Bert) Wilcock. As a strike duo they repeatedly destroyed opposition batting orders and at the end of the 1948 season both players finished with an identical League bowling average: 71 wickets each at a cost of only 475 runs for an average of 6.69. A truly remarkable average for a single bowler in any team, but for both bowlers to record identical analysis is an even more remarkable and surely unique cricket record.

Lean times befell the club on and off the field in the latter part of the century, but at the dawn of the new Millennium the club members rallied and made great efforts and with the help of the National Lottery and other local bodies generously supporting them, opened a superb pavilion complex with unrivalled player facilities, a large club room with bar and catering which will serve the club well into the next century. With this impetus successful times returned to the club on the field with a dominant period of trophy success at senior and junior level throughout the middle of the next decade. After a brief hiccup in this form the 1st XI are now back in the Premier Division of the Halifax Cricket League for the new season and looking forward to further successes. No doubt the present captain will be hoping the legend that is Charlie Pugh and Bert Wilcock will be re-born on the square at Ewood Holmes during 2013 and for many years to come.

1948 Winners Halifax Cricket League First Division - 1st XI Bowling prize
Identical Analysis   71 wkts   475 runs   Ave 6.69.

A magnificent performance in itself to take 71 wkts at 6.69.

A truly remarkable and surely unique record to share this with a team mate at the same club.

## NORTHOWRAM HEDGE TOP CRICKET CLUB

Northowram Hedge Top are a fine example of how a club has developed and improved itself while it has been a member of the Halifax Cricket League.

Facility development on a 'self-help' basis has been a major part of the club's portfolio, beginning in 1968 with the construction of covered 'flush' toilet facilities. A new brick pavilion was constructed in 1980, which was later extended to include showering, toilet and social facilities. These on-site developments have continued into the 21st century ensuring that the venue is recognised as one of the best-appointed in the Halifax Cricket League.

Although the club has had an under-18 team since the early 1950s, the real momentum in youth cricket has been achieved over the last twenty years so that the club is now represented at under-11, 13, 15 and 17. This investment quickly paid rich dividends, not merely in terms of winning trophies, which have been abundant, but also in ensuring that the club has a continuing source of young players. The introduction of a team into the Halifax League's Sunday Section in 1991 has also proved to be an ideal vehicle for introducing the promising youngsters into open-age cricket.

Over the decades Northowram Hedge Top Cricket Club has always had a dedicated core of committed members typified, in leadership terms, by the records of Walter Howden and Harry Andrews. Walter Howden served the club in many capacities from 1935 to 1982 and became a hands-on President from 1983 to 1991. Harry Andrew was captain of the 1st team from 1961-64 and again in 1974. After a short period as Secretary, he was Treasurer for 30 years and retired in 1998 to become a working President, a post he filled for 12 years. These men were Hedge Top to the core, personifying the values that have seen the club arrive at where it is today.

*Bruce M. Deadman*

## OLD CROSSLEYANS CRICKET CLUB

When you visit the headquarters of Old Crossleyans Cricket Club out of season, you are greeted by an interesting sight: rugby posts, rugby-pitch markings that overlap with cricket-pitch markings, and a fluorescent orange 'fence' that guards the out-of-use cricket square.

Old Crossleyans are a hybrid organisation: they are mainly a rugby union club, but also boast a cricket team, a squash side and a junior rugby league XIII. The grandiose clubhouse by the main entrance, Standeven House, serves both sets of players, though given the dimensions of the adjacent field; it would never have to do so simultaneously.

The cricket club was formed in 1976 and has a historic link with what is now the Crossley Heath School, located nearby, just the other side of Skircoat Moor Road. In the early days, it was very much an 'old boys' club, but today probably less than half its members have a connection with the school. As such, it is now an 'open' club and welcomes new members from all over.

Boarders at the school previously resided at Standeven House. What is now the function room and bar used to be the schoolboys' library. Even though the boarders have long since gone, the school still uses Broomfield Avenue for sports fixtures.

The club's Skircoat Green HQ is adjacent to a prep school, The Gleddings, and wedged between the A6026 (Wakefield Road) and the A646 (Skircoat Moor Road). It is close to various other sports fields in and around Savile Park and Manor Heath.

The playing area is surrounded by new houses, trees and bushes. You can also hear the noise of trains entering or exiting Halifax on their way from Manchester to Bradford or Bradford to Manchester.

Club president Adrian Moore says that Old Crossleyans is one of the youngest clubs in the area. He also reckons that the venue is unique: 'I would hazard a guess that it is the biggest in the Halifax League in terms of playing area and as such are very proud of their ground. On occasions, opposition teams complain that the boundaries are too long.'

He goes on: 'Sometimes, at the start of a season, we have to bring the boundary markers in a few yards, to enable maintenance work to take place on the field, and even then some teams complain. Given the current points system in operation, which rewards high totals, I'm sure other sides, based at smaller venues, have an advantage!'

Moore is happy with the square: 'Our groundsman takes a lot of care over the wicket, and it's a good batting track. We've certainly had no complaints.'

Old Crossleyans can boast that the England Rugby Union player Brian Moore played here for 3 seasons. A rugby union player first and foremost but he wasn't a bad cricketer at all. Club stalwart Geoff Manger's claim to fame was that when Geoff was captain of the 2nd XI he actually played with Brian.

## OLD TOWN CRICKET CLUB

'It's up there somewhere, but don't ask me exactly where!' so said the female pedestrian on Burnley Road in the middle of Hebden Bridge.

For the first-time visitor, locating the village of Old Town, never mind the headquarters of Old Town CC, can be a nightmare. The place is easy enough to locate on a map: up from Hebden Bridge, and lying equidistant from Midgehole to the west and Chisley to the east. Old Town is one of the highest cricket venues in the area.

The old pavilion, opened on 8 June 1957 had served the club well but it was replaced with a splendid new building in 1991.

The brick scorebox was built in the late 1990's at a cost of £10,000. There are neat wheeled sightscreens too, which during the close-season, remain in place, but the white sheeting is taken out.

There's also a huge chimney in the near distance, connected to what used to be Mitchell's mill. It was built in 1890 and overlooks the ground when one exits the ground, one can do so via the 'OTCC' gates to the right of the pavilion. The gates are made out of iron and look rather smart.

Boston Hill can get pretty wild. Even though trees line the ground, the wind can really get up, and in September, as the Halifax Cricket League season draws to a close, the playing area can sometimes attract a carpet of golden-coloured autumnal leaves. It can also get quite foggy.

Old Town CC was formed as far back as 1885, although it temporarily disbanded between 1891 and 1894. Originally, it played its home games at Middle Nook Farm on the far eastern fringes of the village. In time, the farm became the site of a house called 'Stalheim', now known as 'Burnside'.

In 1895, it moved to Old Laithe, in the Chisley area. In Old Town Cricket Club: A Short History, this ground is described in the following terms: 'It was in a bleak and isolated position, 1,100 feet above sea level, occupying one of the last flat patches of land before the moors started'.

During the Second World War, Old Laithe was requisitioned by the National Fire Service - with compensation duly paid to the club.

After the war, the club announced the formation of a special sub-committee, 'for the purpose of securing a field more convenient'. The feeling was that Old Laithe was too small and the pitch too uneven. The official history says: 'Conditions were very spartan. Water had to be brought to the ground for each match and toilet facilities were distinctly elementary. Something better was needed!'

Finally, in 1957, the club relocated to Boston Hill. In June 1957 the ground was officially opened by Lord Trefgarne of the National Playing Fields' Association. He declared: 'It is the opinion of our headquarters that the creation of this cricket field is one of the finest voluntary efforts which has come before them.'

Boston Hill was christened on 27 April 1957, with Old Town 2nd XI taking on Stones 2nd XI. The year after, Old Town spent an unhappy year in the Halifax Amateur League, and the year after that, it joined the Halifax Cricket League. The new ground not only hosted cricket but the Whit Monday Gala - a big local event - and various functions and dinner dances, many of which were fundraisers for OTCC.

In the early days, Old Town elevens competed in the Calder Valley League and the Hebden Bridge League, and in 1895 five members of the local Greenwood family turned out for the first team. Times were hard: in 1906, after journeying to Cragg Vale in a specially-hired wagonette, the Old Town 1st XI was skittled out for a paltry total of 11.

It's a nice place to play cricket. It's also a lovely place to watch the game. On a good day, you can sit in the pavilion, or on the veranda, and look down towards the action. Some grounds you're on the same level; here you're almost on top of the cricket. One home supporter declares: 'I might be biased, but at Old Town you get a beautiful setting and good facilities.'

## OUTLANE CRICKET CLUB

Outlane CC was formed in 1897 and was known originally as Outlane Methodist New Connexion Cricket Club. It became Outlane CC in 1919.

Between 1897 and 1920, the club played in the Huddersfield and District Junior League; between 1921 and 1973 Huddersfield and District Cricket Association; and since 1974 in the Halifax Cricket League.

Outlane has had three grounds. The first was behind what is now the Old Golf House Hotel (where the motorway is) and rent was paid to the 'Board of Guardians'.

The building that is now the Old Golf House Hotel was built as a children's home (c.1905) and subsequently became the Golf Club headquarters. Clearly some of the money paid to the landlord for rent was recovered by sub-letting the ground for pasture.

At the Annual General Meeting on 6 November 1928, the Board of Guardians informed the meeting that the field had been sold to Outlane Golf Club.

However, on the 12 December 1928, Mr Noble had negotiated with Mr Saxton that the club could rent a field from him for £10 per year and though the club asked for a 10-year lease, this was not granted. During February and March of 1929, Mr Pugh was asked to lay a wicket.

A quarter of a mile of class-28 wire was purchased from David Green of Lytham, 50 posts at 1/- were purchased and 20 yards of canvas for sightscreens were obtained from Spratt's.

The old pavilion was pulled down on 2 March 1929. The new field was situated at the rear of where Saxton's Garage is now (Cote Farm) and on the 7 May 1929 it was resolved that golf would no longer be allowed to be played on the field.

Early in 1929 the club moved to its second home – Cote Farm. On 1 October 1934 it was resolved that the club leave Cote Farm for Lindley Moor – its present home, and on 15 December 1934 a meeting was arranged at Lindley Moor to view the proposal.

On 9 December 1935 the old pavilion at Cote Farm was pulled down and rebuilt at Lindley Moor and in May 1935 a concrete practice wicket was laid at the new ground.
If there was ever an award for the 'British Cricket Ground Situated Closest to a Motorway', Outlane would be clear favourites.

In the Calderdale region, Rastrick CC and Blackley CC would push them close, but Outlane would just have the edge. Their table-top, motorway-adjacent HQ lies just yards from the M62 and also just yards away from the boundary with Kirklees.

Outlane cricketers explain that they quickly get used to the motorway noise - and that they get withdrawal symptoms when they don't hear the rush of traffic at away venues - but for the first-time visitor to the ground, the motorway noise is the first thing that one notices.

The ground is perched at a pretty high level and from the top perimeter fence one can see for miles and miles into the distance.

To the right one can make out the small green and white arena that is Blackley Cricket Club, and straight ahead one can just deduce where Elland Cricket Club and Elland Golf Club are situated. Outlane is a well-run club, as evidenced by the fact that it has attracted a range of local advertisers. The location is ideal and the big, colourful advertising wall hoardings can be seen by all who travel in the Leeds direction on the very nearby M62.

## OXENHOPE CRICKET CLUB

Oxenhope Cricket Club have been members of the Halifax Cricket League since 2004 and in that time the club has transformed their facilities including a new clubhouse and in February 2013 the village cricket club got the go ahead for a vital project to further expand its facilities.

Oxenhope Cricket Club is based on Hebden Bridge Road, but limited facilities meant they had to play on the same field they practice on. Home to eight teams, this means the club struggled to keep the pitch in pristine condition.

Already supported by Oxenhope Parish Council, the club has been granted permission by Bradford Council to build practice nets on a neighbouring field, part of Oxenhope Primary School and near the village community centre.

The club's chairman confirmed that the nets will make the club more sustainable for the future, and would be open for use by the school and other village groups.

Derrick Hopkinson was reported saying that: "At the moment the teams have to practice on the current square. It is just not sustainable for us to do that, especially with poor weather. It's not good for the field."

This project will give them some fully enclosed practice nets and ensure sustainable facilities for their Junior and Senior teams in the future.

**CLUB HONOURS**

**1st XI**
**Keighley Cup Winners**
1962  1964  1970 1972  1974  1975  1982  1990
**West Bradford League Winners**
1960  1962  1963  1965  1967  1971  1973
**Bradford Central League Winners**
Division 1 1977    Division 2 1976 1999 2002
**Halifax League Winners**
Division 1 Conference 2006

**2nd XI**
**Keighley Cup Winners**
1948  1951  1960  1972  1982
**West Bradford League Winners**
1956  1960  1971  1973  1974
**Thrippleton Cup Winners**
1978  1996
**Bradford Central League Winners**
Division 2  1999  2002
**Halifax Cricket League Winners**
Division 1 Conference 2006
Division 2 2011

# QUEENSBURY CRICKET CLUB

*First team captain James Myers pictured with the Terry Wynne Second Division Trophy in front of the RD Smith Memorial score box (September 2011)*

Queensbury Cricket Club was formed on 1 January 2000 as a result of the merger of Union Croft and Yews Green cricket clubs. The new club took the name of Queensbury as it was then the only cricket club based in the "village" of Queensbury, and assumed Union Croft's place in the Halifax Cricket League. (It should be noted that there is no connection with the former Bradford League club of the same name).

When formed, the club identified as priorities facilities improvement at the Old Guy Road ground, and the development of a junior section.

The first task undertaken, in January 2000, was the installation of mains water – the previous supply being from a local borehole, and flushing toilets. Since then, a score box & machinery storage area and artificial double bay practice nets have been constructed.

The score box and machinery storage area, winner of the inaugural Huddersfield University "Heritage Award", is dedicated to Richard "RD" Smith – a Queensbury member who collapsed and died whilst playing for the first team at Bridgeholme, and was partly funded by a donation from his widow.

The artificial practice area was supported by the local Councillors (Cllrs Michael Walls, Linda Cromie, & Paul Cromie) and mainly funded by grants from Bradford Council's Single Regeneration budget and from the Queensbury Urban Village. Since the facility was opened, an increasing number of young people have used it both informally and for organised coaching.
The club has also achieved its other initial priority - developing a junior section, and now enters teams in the Bramleys Halifax Junior Cricket League at Under 11, 13, 15, and 17 age groups.

The club has strived to become an important and well respected club within the Halifax Cricket League. Endeavours to improve our playing standards since inception culminated in the first XI winning the Terry Wynne Second Division championship in 2011.

# S.B.C.I. CRICKET CLUB

As its full name suggests, Sowerby Bridge Church Institute Cricket Club owes its existence to the young men of Christ Church, Sowerby Bridge during the 1880s.

The Young Men's Class formed a team to play in the Sowerby Division League, voting against a proposal to pay umpires in 1894, such tradition underpinning many of it's current attitudes!

The team was known as Christ Church CC until 1909 when it became SBCI, presumably following the establishment of the Christ Church Institute, a Church organisation providing social and recreational activity for its congregation. The cricket club is the last remaining arm, as witnessed through the selection of ground trustees from the congregation of the Church.

The Club has played at the Astleys since its purchase in 1921, a ground with superb panoramic views of the surrounding hills and valleys with a reassuring gentle breeze always available to offset the heat of the summer.

Each generation made their own considerable contribution to the development of the club ranging from its first pavilion in 1921 costing £500, through ground levelling in 1959 and mains water in 1984. However, the award of grant funding in the late 90's allowed the transformational change to the facilities enjoyed today.

The new build was part of the development plan started some years earlier which had its foundation in the promotion of junior cricket, resulting in the club currently being recognised as one of the leading lights within the Halifax Cricket League.

It is perhaps appropriate that as we celebrate such a unique event as the League's centenary, SBCI were, in 2012 the proud holders of both the Premiership and Parish Cup trophies for the first time in the clubs history within the Halifax Cricket League, a legacy of the last century perhaps, with 90% of the squad having come through the junior ranks.

## SHELF CRICKET CLUB

In 1856 a team called Shelf Victoria was playing matches at the back of the Shoulder of Mutton Inn. This would be the forerunner to the current Shelf Club which became founder members of the Bradford League in 1903 and became the first Champions.

The club it seems has always played at Carr House Lane and the ground is the fifth highest Calderdale cricket ground in terms of altitude.

In 2002, the Shelf ground was the scene of unprecedented development work. Out went the old, increasingly dilapidated pavilion; and in came two semi-permanent steel portakabins. Malcolm Walker, a member of the club committee, explained: 'We had to do it - the old building had been falling down for a number of years. It was definitely on its last legs.'

He goes on to describe a common problem: '"For a small club like ours, we just didn't have the time or the expertise to put together a full business plan and then apply for grants and funding. It was too much work. We've got enough on our plate just existing, and trying all the time to attract new members.

So we decided on the two-portakabins idea as a halfway house. These were converted into changing rooms and a tea room. They're as permanent as they need to be and we raised a lot of cash to afford them."'

These facilities, which were only intended to be a temporary measure, were to be replaced when the club gained approval from planning chiefs in 2011.There has been much hard work for the club since these plans were passed.

Since joining the Halifax League in 2007 the second team won the second division championship in that first year and followed up in 2010 by being champions of the first division. In 2010 the first team claimed the Lindley Moor Trophy. After those initial years of success we now find both our teams back in their respective second divisions.

## SOUTHOWRAM CRICKET CLUB

The 'new' Southowram CC was originally a pub team based at The Cock and Bottle, at the other end of the village.

Club spokesman Keith Walker says: 'The ground we've got today was once a quarried tip. It was converted into a cricket ground and then leased from Marshall's, a local company. At first, the pavilion was a hut, but in 1990, with the financial assistance of the Sports Foundation, members of the club erected the pavilion that stands there today.'

In recent years, other work has been undertaken at the ground. At the end of the 1990s the whole playing area was 're-levelled' and in 2002 a new wicket was laid.

Walker says the square has always been good: 'I would say that at one point, it was the fairest in the League. We dug it up, flattened it out, and now it's both fast and true. And all the plaudits have got to go to former groundsman Mick Pollard.'

Ashday Lane is also unique. It was the first ground in the Halifax Cricket League to witness six sixes being hit in the same over.

The year: 2001. The opposition: Greetland. The man with the muscles: Fiaz Haider.

The cricket ground lies far off the beaten track. Indeed, as one looks out from the pavilion, one can see no other buildings at all - except for a plethora of large steel pylons.

Ashday Hall - whose history goes as far back as 1275 - is just up the road, but the residential areas of Southowram are nowhere to be seen.

This is the venue's chief charm - the serenity that envelops the arena.

The ground is extremely well appointed.

The Southowram CC website states, 'Facilities: Rollers, Changing Facilities, Pavilion, Score Box', but this, of course, does not tell the whole story.

The playing surface is of a good size and there are several pitches for captain and groundsman to choose from (in high summer the strips can look very parched).

The person who cuts the outfield does so very effectively, and also creates some pretty 'mowing' patterns in the process.

In addition, the sightscreens are definitely above average in quality.

One Halifax League player says: 'It's a nice ground to play at - the facilities are good but there is a downward slope to the playing area that makes things slightly tricky.'

There are baskets of colourful flowers by the pavilion - a nice touch - but the most appealing aspect of the ground, apart from its almost timeless, semi-rural location, is the seating: seven brown-and-white wooden benches to the left of the pavilion, double that amount to the right, and four more perched in front of the pavilion.

The seats are not just attractive in themselves, but together give the venue a relaxed feel and a pleasant aura.

The pavilion is akin to a large modern bungalow. When there's no cricket going on, it is shuttered up, but the blue and yellow 'Southowram CC' flag flutters continually from the roof - signposting a highly impressive local landmark.

In 2002, Southowram CC celebrated their 25th anniversary year by winning the right to host the Parish Cup final. (The club's 1st XI actually battled their way through to the final - so they had the bonus of home advantage).

However, after days of torrential rain, the showpiece fixture had to be postponed a week - a huge disappointment for club officials, who had already ordered extra toilets for the big occasion from Leeds!

## SOWERBY BRIDGE CC

According to one source: 'Sowerby Bridge was very much a creation of the Industrial Revolution'. Over the years the town has gained a reputation for the manufacture of cloth, iron and toffees. It was also a key interchange for trains, buses and trams.

In a hidden corner of Sowerby Bridge - wedged between a factory complex, a beautiful sweep of greenery, and a narrow stretch of the meandering River Calder - lies a neat, flat, compact and rather distinguished cricketing venue, which was bought by Sowerby Bridge CC almost two-thirds of a century ago, in July 1936. It is only a six-hit away from the main Halifax-Rochdale road, but it is a peaceful, secluded place.

Granted, at the pavilion end, it is difficult to escape industrial noise, but around the other three sides of the ground, town becomes country: from west to east - a tree-lined mount, with the odd red and purple flower to add a dash of colour; a farmer's field, complete with busy tractor; and a grassy river bank, with water trickling gently below ('THE RYBURN ANGLING SOCIETY LIMIT' pronounces an A4 notice pinned to a protruding tree).

The river is a key feature of the venue: 'A lot of balls end up in the water, but we're pretty ingenuous in recovering them. At one point we used a fishing net; then we trained a member's dog to fish them out; and now we're using modern technology - a remote-control toy boat that is very good at detecting small round red things!'

A seasoned visitor to Sowerby Bridge says: 'It's an unusual setting, but the facilities are good and you really feel involved in the game. It's also a good place for a walk - sometimes it's nice to dip in and out of the game.'

The pavilion, to the right as one enters the ground through the main entrance, is brown and tan in colour: there are five (protected) windows, three brown doors and two sets of steps. The building was rebuilt in 1985 after a fire the year before, and it fits in nicely with the architecture of the Calder Valley as a whole.

The original scorebox was erected in 1934; today, a simple scoreboard is incorporated into the frontage of the new pavilion. A visiting player comments: 'The playing area is flat and large. There are good photos of the Sowerby Bridge floods inside the clubhouse and the club is also famous for Richard Sladdin, who went on to play for Derbyshire.'

Sowerby Bridge CC has a long history. It was founded in 1852, and thus celebrated its 150th anniversary in 2002. In its early years, it played at Fore Lane - halfway between Sowerby Bridge and Sowerby - and another venue in the town, just off Burnley Road.

The club moved to its current headquarters in the period immediately following the end of the Great War, and purchased it in 1936. During the Second World War, the ground was used by the War Office as a detention barracks or prison.

As such, the club had to find an alternative venue for its wartime fixtures, and so it lodged temporarily at Sowerby St. Peter's CC, up the hill in Sowerby village. Because of the 'merging' of the two clubs between 1939 and 1945, when the war finally ended, some Sowerby Bridge players switched to the St. Peter's club and some players from St. Peter's moved in the opposite direction.

The war may have finished in 1945, but it took time for Sowerby Bridge's ground to revert back to its normal use. In May 1947, a town meeting demanded that the War Office move out, but this did not happen until February the following year. By April 1950 - a full five years after the war ended - it was finally back as a venue for local league cricket.

The ground boasts one orthodox sightscreen (at the far end) and one long white wall that doubles as the batsmen's friend (at the other). But at Sowerby Bridge's HQ, the main issue isn't seeing the ball, but finding it if it's ever hoisted out of sight. It either lands in the river, in the middle of bushes, or on top of a very elongated factory roof.

The ground scores well in terms of serenity and facilities. The wicket here is one of the best in the League and a team batting first would generally be looking to post a total around the 200 mark. The club hosts the Parish Cup final every four or five years, and Sowerby Bridge is one of the top five grounds in the Halifax Cricket League.'

## SOWERBY ST PETER'S CC

Sowerby St. Peter's Cricket Club were not founder members of the Halifax Parish League, as they joined the League in 1923 nine years after the League was formed.

Both club sides won their respective League titles in the Halifax and District League in 1922 before joining the Halifax Parish League the following year, enjoying early success by winning the Parish Cup in 1926, beating Illingworth in the final at Thrum Hall.

Early in the 20th century the ground was levelled by reducing the slope at the top end of the ground. The amenities of the club were housed in several green painted wooden huts.

During the second World War the club shared its ground with neighbours Sowerby Bridge CC whose ground was being used as a prison camp.

Revenue was raised by holding social functions in the local church hall until in the 1960's the club purchased a wooden hut from the RAF in York and this became the main clubhouse for changing rooms and catering facilities as well as providing facilities to hold family and other functions for the local community. An extension was added in 1985 and the club refurbished and re-opened in 1988. Revenue from the bar was used to build a new scorebox which today houses an electric scoreboard, and the club employs a professional groundsman who enables it to host the Parish Cup Final in rotation with a number of other clubs. The ground is also used for Yorkshire County games at junior level.

On the playing side the 1st team has won the League title on six occasions in the last 50 years as well as winning the Parish Cup five times since joining the League. The second eleven first won the League title in 1940 and in a 30 year period from 1951 won the League title on thirteen occasions as well as winning the Crossley Shield five times, having a very strong team during that period. They have since won the Crossley Shield in 2002 and 2011 and the club Sunday Section team won the League Cup in 2012.

Today the club runs three senior teams as well as several junior teams in the Halifax Cricket League and their facilities are considered to be amongst the best in the League. The club is planning to extend the pavilion as well as maintaining ties with local schools who also use the club facilities. The junior section of the club is very healthy and this will ensure that the club continues the work done by previous generations.

## STAINLAND CRICKET CLUB

John Wesley visited the place in 1759, the Halifax Permanent Building Society opened a Stainland branch in 1855, and in the early twentieth century, villagers succumbed to two nasty epidemics (mumps - 1907; scarlet fever - 1912). These events apart, things have always remained pretty quiet in Stainland.

When one jumps off the bus in the centre of Stainland, one is swiftly acquainted with all the hallmarks of a quintessential Yorkshire village: the parish church, the two public houses, the general store and the charming old fashioned cottages that line the narrow and meandering main street (one actually dates from 1703). Then there's the cricket ground.

Stainland's home patch is set back a few hundred yards from the road, beyond the Red Lion pub, the adjoining car park and the pretty, flower-adorned bowling green that backs onto the cricket ground. There are also swings, slides and tennis courts nearby.The main road feels a long distance away from the cricket field - all that can be heard is the gentle buzz of cars and buses travelling to and from Holywell Green and Sowood.

In many ways it is the archetypal village cricket venue: a low, semi-whitewashed dry stone wall at one end, a herd of cows wandering aimlessly in a large adjacent field, and vast swathes of farmland for almost as far as the eye can see. Almost all the benches round the ground's perimeter are dedicated to friends and followers of the team.

Stainland CC was established in 1884. For the best part of 40 years, they played at Drury Lane - a venue famous for its bandstand. In 1922, the club received their current ground, on Stainland Road, as a post-war gift. The working men of the village had a new recreation area, and the folk at the British Legion were named as trustees.

The Memorial Ground, a peaceful, semi-rural setting, now boasts a spanking new beige-and-green pavilion (which is also utilised by the hardworking bowls players when they are in action).

Club secretary Paul Carter explains: 'Fire ripped down the old building in 1996. In the years that followed we had to decide what to do. The council provided us with some temporary changing facilities and a portakabin to use as a tea room, but we had to think long-term. We applied for Lottery funding, with other sports organisations in the village, but all our applications failed.' In the end, the cricket club decided to go it alone, and by May 2001 a permanent building had been erected and officially opened. There is a nice symbolic touch in that the Stainland CC badge is painted onto the pavilion front, a white rose against a yellow and blue background.

From the middle, one can see the town-centre office blocks of Halifax on the far horizon, the ornate architecture of Stainland church only a few hundred yards away, and Blackley CC's hillside ground in the medium distance. (Stainland players declare that Blackley and Outlane are the two big local rivals; they say the rivalry with Greetland 'is not as intense').

Stainland have never won the Halifax Cricket League, but they did claim the Division 2 title in 1979 and, more recently, in 2002. Their ground is one of the biggest in the Halifax Cricket League and is very flat.

## STONES CRICKET CLUB – A BRIEF HISTORY

The club was formed in 1884 and were called Stones Wesleyan Cricket Club. The name was taken because the team was formed from the congregation of the then Stones Wesleyan Methodist Church. They first played in a field opposite the Stones Chapel and this field can still be viewed today and it is noticeable where the wicket was because it had been dug out from the sloping field to leave a visible ledge.

The small village of Ripponden was divided up into smaller districts that each provided their own entertainment and activities which were centred on the churches and chapels and each one had a cricket team. In Ripponden there were six teams, Barkisland, Ripponden Conservative Club, Rishworth, Soyland Town, Stones and Zion all playing in the Halifax & District Amateur League. There was always quite a stir when the teams happened to meet each other. In 1919 when Stones met Rishworth in a final it appears that Rishworth were very confident of success. Rishworth Band was going to be on hand at Ripponden after the match to parade the team and Cup back to Rishworth. At the interval all seemed to be going to plan with Stones being bowled out for 34 but Stones then bowled out Rishworth for 24 and the Rishworth band had to accompany Stones and the Cup up Rochdale Road instead of going along Oldham Road to Rishworth!

The club, after the First World War, moved up to their current ground at Swift Cross, Ripponden Old Lane which is situated high above Ripponden. As one navigates any of the meandering hillside lanes en route to the ground one does begin to wonder whether it exists at all, however, just before desperation sets in, it comes into view.

The ground was rented at first, then in 1924, the club was given the opportunity to buy the ground for £100. Four trustees each chipped in with £25 each to purchase the land from J R Whiteley at Great House and the club asset remains in the hands of four trustees to this very day.

The club changed its name to Stones Methodist CC in the early 1930's and joined the Halifax League at the AGM in 1936 (See the September 1936 Stones AGM Minute confirming application to the League). This name lasted into the early 1970's when the club became known as Stones

Cricket Club but the club cheque book still states Stones Methodist CC. Swift Cross is full of curiosities. In the 1920's and 1930's it was not just the site of a cricket ground but there was also a putting green and a set of tennis courts to keep the locals occupied in their small window of leisure time available in those days. The ground was also famous for being narrow and having long grass. Boundaries in those days were two's and four's and white lines were marked on the walls opposite the creases so that in between the boundaries were twos and behind the stumps were fours! The small ground problem was rectified in the very early 1960's when the club widen the field on both sides by arrangement with the local farmer Mr Crowther on one side, and by purchasing land from a Mr Ellsworth on the other side. 2,400 square yards were bought at a cost of £60 which was a great deal of money back in 1960. More land could have been bought because Mr Ellsworth said the club could have as much as they like but the club could not afford.

The club also has witnessed many changes on and around the boundary's edge. In the 1930's the club erected a wooden tea hut, near where the scorebox is situated today, which came all the way from the Shay Football Stadium. The pavilion up to 1971 was a corrugated iron building which offered little protection or comfort to the players. A new stone pavilion was constructed by volunteering members, and a match between Stones and a Halifax League President's XI was staged to mark this very special occasion.

24 years later the club was able to unveil another new pavilion and this was officially opened on the 15 July 1995 by fast bowler Peter Lever. This pavilion was further enhanced and improved in time for the 125th anniversary of the club in 2009. The stone scorebox arrived in 1972 and is dedicated to Harold Whitehead, who not only was a long serving member of the club and held office as both Chairman and President, but was also the League President from 1946 to 1964.

There also has to be a special mention, in a brief history of Stones Cricket Club, to Kenny Brown for his dedication, effort, time and enthusiasm that he gave to the club over his lifetime. He was a good player opening the batting for many years, scoring many 50's, a top score of 133 down at Copley and played a major role in both Parish Cup wins in 1938 and 1954. He was club Secretary for 30 years, then Chairman and finally President. He was the club League Representative and held a position on the League Executive. Kenny was involved with all the work that went on, with every project overseeing the club facilities being transformed from a hen pen to a cricket ground that everyone could be very proud of. The iron gates at the main entrance are a fitting memorial to Kenny whose dedication to the club is a fine example to everyone of how individuals have contributed to their clubs over the past 100 years.

*David Normanton - Stones CC - Treasurer*

Annual General Meeting held
28ᵗʰ. Sept. 1936, in Stones School.
Mr. H. Habergham in the chair.

Pro. & Sec. That the minutes of the last Annual
General Meeting held 7ᵗʰ Oct. 1936 be
passed as read.

" " That the Balance Sheet be adopted
as read by the Financial Secretary.

" " That we send a letter conveying our
best thanks to Mrs Palmer for assisting
in selling refreshments throughout
the year.

" " A vote of thanks & was passed to Mrs.
Pearson and all ladies who helped with
the refreshments during the season.

" " That the committee's action in continuing
in the Halifax Parish Cup Competition
be confirmed.

" " That we apply for admission into
the Halifax Cricket League.

" " That we enter a third team in the
Y.M.C.A. Red Triangle League under 18
on condition that the type of play

to be used in 1937 is suitable. The
committee to decide in this matter.
For & Sec. The following we elected officials
for 1937.
President. Miss. S. Barlett
Patrons. The following to be approached
together with last years list.
Miss. Wrangham. & Messrs. J. Dyson.
J. Whiteley. J. Hirst & W. Edge.
Secretary. A. Howarth.
Financial Secretary. S. Pearson.
Treasurer J. Holroyde.
Representatives. to League Meetings. Secretary.
to Halifax Parish Cup. Comp. Mr. S. Pearson.
To Red Triangle League. Mr. G. Hamer.
Honorary Subscriptions Collectors. Messrs. G. Hamer
& H. Whiteley.
Auditors. Messrs. F. Beverley & G. Eastwood.
General Committee.
Messrs. S. Firth, W. Whiteley, W. Cole,
H. Whiteley, N. Crowther, L. Holland,
S. Palmer, A. Pearson, S. Pearson, G. Hamer
& D. Hamer.

Stones Cricket Club - Minute Book Extract 1937

Pro. Sec. That the matter of repair to, and painting of Pavilion be left till the end of the season.

"     "    That Secretary tries to get wash basin for visitor's hut.

"     "    That we have 1st & 2nd Team fixtures printed as soon as possible.

"     "    That we write Hebble re 'bus to take teams to opponents grounds.

"     "    That the following be appointed official scorers for 1937. 1st Team B. Crawshaw. 2nd Team. R. Graham.

"     "    That we purchase 3 pairs of Batting Pads. + Wisden Grade A. Balls, + 2 full size Body guards.

"     "    That the matter of Pencils and Recipe Books be left to a later date.

"     "    That Mr. S. Pearson be left to appoint a ladies' committee.

"     "    That the next meeting be held on Monday 19th April at 8. p. m.

W Cox

MAY 1937

# THE HALIFAX DAILY COURIER

## PELLON

# Local Clubs Win Brilliantly.

## Halifax and King Cross Excel.

### Great Century by Radcliffe.

#### RESULTS AT A GLANCE.

Halifax beat Rotherham by 19 runs.
King Cross beat Whitwood by eight wickets.
Sowerby Bridge beat Steeton by 44 runs.
Elland beat Golcar by five wickets.
Rastrick beat Honley by six wickets.
Saltaire v. Brighouse drawn.

Cricket can be a highly exhilarating spectacle when played in the right spirit and no club in the Yorkshire League has done more to make the summer pastime a thrilling sport than the Halifax side during the past few seasons. Against Rotherham they provided another excellent match with the result in doubt to the final minutes and Rotherham were only beaten five minutes before stumps were due to be drawn.

It was indeed a fine performance on the part of the Thrum Hall men to beat the strong Rotherham side, and at the same time a praiseworthy effort on the part of Rotherham to knock off the runs after a disastrous start.

#### MASTERFUL DISPLAY.

Halifax, however, owed much to the brilliant display of Leonard Radcliffe, who commenced the home innings and was undefeated for 107 when the declaration was made. In a game which was characterised by several good individual efforts, Radcliffe's innings eclipsed them all, for, apart from two difficult chances he was easily superior to the best of the Rotherham attack. From the very outset he displayed all his old confidence, and once he had reached the 50 mark he began to give the attack and the crowd a taste of his real powers. Boundary hits simply flowed from his bat and nearly half his runs were scored by this means. He emphasised the fact that he is still one of the League's best batsmen.

His grand hitting put Halifax on the high road to victory, though praise is due too to Helliwell for his valuable help, which enabled the side to declare at 189 for the loss of five wickets.

#### DURKIN TO THE RESCUE.

Rotherham commenced badly by losing Heaton with only a single in the score book, but they have a strong batting side and White and Smith soon made it apparent that Halifax were faced with a severe task.

By means of entertaining cricket, both topped the half-century, and made victory possible for the visitors. E. J. Durkin, however, had other ideas, for no one better than the slow left hander loves a tilt at the "big-hitters." Coming on for the second time he commenced a devastating spell which was not ended until his last ball hit the bails of Douglas's

---

fifth wicket stand of 83. A big factor in the victory of Elland was the fine bowling of the professional, W. Dennis, who finished with the good figures of six for 34.

#### WADE'S SPLENDID INNINGS.

A feature of the Brighouse and Saltaire match was the great innings of M. T. Wade, the former King Cross player and Yorkshire colt. Wade, who is a pupil of Herbert Sutcliffe, scored 95 of his side's total of 200 for seven wickets. His innings was noted for excellent driving and leg hitting. He had most assistance from A. Higson (31) and H. Gill (44 not out). Saltaire, who batted first, made 208 for nine. Chief contributors were J. H. Ellicot (47 not out) and E. A. Hutton (39).

### YORKSHIRE LEAGUE.

#### HALIFAX v. ROTHERHAM.

Halifax 189 for 5, dec.—L. Radcliffe not out 107, F. H. Taylor c White b Hampshire 13, F. Symons run out 1, J. Speak b Hampshire 7, J. Gledhill st White b Stainrod 16, T. Helliwell c Smith b Mosely 38, R. Wadsworth not out 2, extras 5.

Rotherham. 168.—L. Leadbeater lbw b Helliwell 9, C. Heaton b Gledhill 0, S. White c Wadsworth b Durkin 63, G. Carr b Helliwell 6, E. W. Smith c Radcliffe b Durkin 71, H. B. Mosely b Durkin 0, J. Hampshire b Durkin 4, R. E. Parkin c Charnock b Gledhill 4, A. P. Stainrod st Holroyd b Durkin 2, R. H. Douglas b Durkin 6, R. L. Grogat not out 0, extras 3.

#### WHITWOOD v. KING CROSS.

Whitwood, 112.—L. Crozier b Crossley 27, R. P. Tordoff c Kippax b Crossley 11, G. Cawthray b Crossley 16, K. S. Brookes lbw b Crossley 2, S. Pickles lbw b Jowitt 1, H. Wailes b Jowitt 0, E. Rollins c Bain b Jowitt 6, W. Baker b Jowitt 5, C. Gill run out 28, T. Mason lbw b Jowitt 1, P. Lunn not out 13, extras 2.

King Cross, 117 for 2.—E. W. King not out 56, K. L. Thomas b Wailes 18, D. E. Jowitt c Pickles b Brookes 30, J. M. Crossley not out 4, extras 9.

#### LEAGUE TABLE.

| | P. | W. | L. | D. | Pts. |
|---|---|---|---|---|---|
| York | 6 | 5 | 1 | 0 | 15 |
| Hull | 7 | 4 | 1 | 2 | 14 |
| King Cross | 6 | 4 | 2 | 0 | 12 |
| Rotherham | 6 | 4 | 2 | 0 | 12 |
| Sheffield United | 7 | 4 | 3 | 0 | 12 |
| Halifax | 6 | 3 | 2 | 1 | 10 |
| Leeds | 6 | 2 | 2 | 2 | 8 |
| Castleford | 6 | 1 | 3 | 2 | 4 |
| Barnsley | 6 | 1 | 5 | 0 | 3 |
| Wakefield | 6 | 0 | 4 | 2 | 2 |
| Doncaster | 6 | 0 | 5 | 1 | 1 |
| Whitwood Coll. | 6 | 0 | 6 | 0 | 0 |

### YORKSHIRE COUNCIL.

#### SOWERBY BRIDGE v. STEETON.

Sowerby Bridge, 128.—G. L. Lawrence c Hill b T. Shackleton 12, E. Graydon b T. Shackleton 9, J. Hartley c Buckle b T. Shackleton 1, W. N. Holden c J. Battersby b Buckle 48, A. Bruce c A. Battersby b Briggs 4, J. E. Eastwood c A. Battersby b Buckle 31, C. Hellawell c J. Battersby b T. Shackleton 6, A. Hodgson b T. Shackleton 5, V. Kenny not out 1, R. Morley c C. Shackleton b T. Shackleton 1, S. Farrar b T. Shackleton 0, extras 10.

Steeton, 84.—J. Battersby c C. Hellawell b Hodgson 11, A. Battersby c Eastwood b Hodgson 25, S. Briggs c Lawrence b Hodgson 3, J. Shackleton lbw b Hodgson 0, W. L. Shackleton c Holden b Hodgson 9, E. Shackleton c Hartley b Farrar 0, R. Nelson c Eastwood b Hodgson 5, C. Shackleton not out 17, R. Lingard b Farrar 4, D. Hill lbw b Holden 3, W. Buckle b Holden 4,

---

Some of the oldest guests being wel

Hume 21, H. Pickles b Wright 1, T. Nicholl c Scott b Wright 0, A. Varley c W. Crossley b Scott 37, F. Wolfenden c Scott b Hume 10, R. W. Broadley b Hume 6, L. Farrar c Wright b Hume 7, M. Culpan c A. Crossley b Hume 8, E. Whiteley lbw b Wright 2, W. Culpan c A. Crossley b Hume 1, P. Farrar not out 5, extras 5.

#### COPLEY v. GREETLAND.

Greetland, 144.—F. Webster b Robinson 30, D. Crossley c Turner b John Nash 51, F. Blagborough b Robinson 24, G. Feavers b John Nash 0, N. Saville b John Nash 2, H. Crowther c R. Smith b Robinson 5, J. Hayes b John Nash 0, W. Crossley run out 0, S. Evans c A. Smith b Robinson 5, S. Layfield c James Nash b Barker 9, S. Thwaites not out 4, extras 14.

Copley, 146 for 3.—James Nash b Layfield 15, K. Taylor not out 42, R. Smith c Layfield b Webster 2, A. Smith b Evans 77, J. Robinson not out 3, extras 7.

#### TURNWRIGHT'S AND CLIFTON v. STONES.

Stones 91.—L. Holland b Irvine 1, L. Palmer b Mellor 2, D. Hamer b Irvine 8, F. Holmes lbw b Irvine 15, D. Nairn b Irvine 1, E. Shaw c Fearnley b Irvine 16, C. Clay b Mello r17, K. Brown b Irvine 29, G. Hamer lbw b Fearnley 0, A. Bottomley b Irvine 0, G. Eastwood not out 1, extras 1.

Turnwright's and Clifton, 94 for 5.—H. Stead not out 32, W. Gooder c and b Eastwood 0, J. Pearson lbw b Clay 21, N. Ingham lbw b Hamer 17, W. Berry b Bottomley 12, F. Robinson c Clay b Bottomley 0, J. Mellor not out 6, extras 6.

#### KING CROSS 2nd v. SALTS 2nd (SALTAIRE).

Salts 2nd 209.—A. Kershaw c Nicholl b Shea 2, G. Smith b Carter (C.) 5, R. Carroll b Shea 5, W. Lightowler c Ellis b Nicholl 53, P. Henry c Goodfellow b Snea 37, E. Abley c Carter (E.) b Ellis 42, E. Tyreman lbw b Wolfenden 26, N. Fazackerley st Walton b Ellis

## STONES METHODIST C. C.

*The Annual Dinner*

*and*

*Presentation of Prizes*

will be held

IN STONES SCHOOL, RIPPONDEN

FRIDAY, 26th NOVEMBER, 1954

at 7-30 p.m. prompt.

Prizes will be presented by

# W. H. FOSTER, Esq.

President of the Bradford Cricket League

TICKETS 4/- EACH.     CHILDREN 2/- EACH.

Stones Methodist Cricket Club.

ANNUAL

## TEA AND CONCERT.

ADULTS' TEA TICKET.

Stones Methodist Cricket Club.

ANNUAL

## TEA AND CONCERT.

Child's Concert Ticket [under 14 yrs.]

STONES METHODIST CRICKET CLUB

# Whist Drive and Dance

IN THE VICTORIA HALL, RIPPONDEN,
SATURDAY, DEC. 20th, 1952.

Whist to commence 6-30 prompt.

Dancing 8-30 to 11-45 p.m.

Music for dancing by
**Tom Mallinson & his Debonaires Orchestra.**
Refreshments at Reasonable Prices.
**Tickets 2/6 each.**
Children half-price.
Old Age Pensioners 2/- at the door.

J. Mellor, Printer, Ripponden.

Name One - Stones Wesleyan Cricket Club

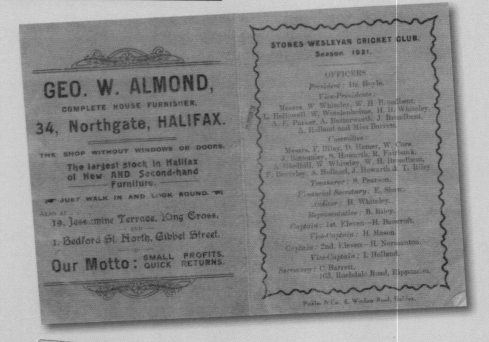

**GEO. W. ALMOND,**
COMPLETE HOUSE FURNISHER,
**34, Northgate, HALIFAX.**

THE SHOP WITHOUT WINDOWS OR DOORS.

The largest stock in Halifax
of New AND Second-hand
Furniture.

JUST WALK IN AND LOOK ROUND.

ALSO AT

19, Jessamine Terrace, King Cross,
AND
1, Bedford St. North, Gibbet Street.

**Our Motto:** SMALL PROFITS.
QUICK RETURNS.

---

**STONES WESLEYAN CRICKET CLUB.**
Season 1921.

OFFICERS

President: Mr. Hoyle.

Vice-Presidents:
Messrs. W. Whiteley, W. H. Broadbent,
L. Hellowell, W. Wotslenholme, H. H. Whiteley,
A. E. Parker, A. Butterworth, J. Broadbent,
A. Holland and Miss Barrett.

Committee:
Messrs. F. Riley, D. Hamer, W. Core,
J. Bottomley, S. Howarth, R. Fairbank,
A. Gledhill, W. Whiteley, W. H. Broadbent,
F. Beverley, A. Holland, J. Howarth & T. Riley.

Treasurer: S. Pearson.

Financial Secretary: E. Shaw.

Auditor: H. Whiteley.

Representative: B. Riley.

Captain: 1st. Eleven—H. Bancroft.
Vice-Captain: H. Mason.

Captain: 2nd. Eleven—H. Normanton.
Vice-Captain: I. Holland.

Secretary: C. Barrett,
103, Rochdale Road, Rippenden.

Parke & Co. 5, Winding Road, Halifax.

---

## Stones Wesleyan Cricket Club.
### FIXTURES FOR SEASON 1921.

**FIRST ELEVEN.**

| Date. Club Played. | Ground. | Result. |
|---|---|---|
| Apr. 30—Heath Old Boys ... | away | |
| May ,7—Luddenden St. Marys | away | |
| ,, 14—Copley ... | home | |
| ,, 21—Rishworth | home | |
| ,, 28—Caddy Field | home | |
| June 4—Booth ... | away | |
| ,, 11— ... | home | |
| ,, 18—Southowram | | |
| ,, 25—Barkisland | home | |
| July 2—Heath Old Boys ... | home | |
| ,, 9—Luddenden St. Marys | home | |
| ,, 16—Copley ... | home | |
| ,, 23—Rishworth | away | |
| ,, 30—Caddy Field | away | |
| Aug. 6— ... | home | |
| ,, 13— | | |
| ,, 20—Booth | | |
| ,, 27— | away | |
| Sept. 3—Southowram | away | |
| ,, 10—Barkisland | away | |

**SECOND ELEVEN.**

| Date. Club played. | Ground. | Result. |
|---|---|---|
| Apr. 30— | | |
| May 7—Luddenden St. Marys | home | |
| ,, 14—Copley ... | away | |
| ,, 21—Rishworth ... | away | |
| ,, 28—Caddy Field ... | home | |
| June 4—Booth | away | |
| ,, 11— | | |
| ,, 18—Southowram | away | |
| ,, 25—Barkisland | away | |
| July 2— | | |
| ,, 9—Luddenden St. Marys | away | |
| ,, 16—Copley ... | home | |
| ,, 23—Rishworth ... | home | |
| May 30—Caddy Field | away | |
| Aug. 6— | | |
| ,, 13— | | |
| ,, 20—Booth | | |
| ,, 27— ... | home | |
| Sept 3—Southowram | home | |
| ,, 10—Barkisland | home | |

## OFFICERS FOR SEASON 1938.

President — Miss S. Barrett.

Chairman — M. S. Pearson.

Honorary Subscribers —
Miss S. Barrett, Jt. Murtagh, Coun. T. H. Foster, Messrs. F. Beverley, J. Beverley, H. Bottomley, H. Crowther, W. B. Edwards, G. K. Garside, J. Gledhill, W. H. Hamer, A. Holliday, I. Howarth, J. Holroyde, S. Howarth, W. H. Lees, A. H. Mallinson, F. Moores, J. Moores, H. Parkes, F. Wolfenden, T. Wattershouse, W. Wattershouse, J. Whiteley, R. Whiteley, W. Whiteley.

Treasurer — Mr. H. Whiteley.

Financial Secretary — Mr. S. Pearson.

Corresponding Secretary — Mr. A. Howarth, 74, New Stones, Ripponden.

Auditors — Messrs. F. Beverley & G. Eastwood.

Selection Committee — H. Habergham, W. Core, N. Crowther, F. Beverley, J. Howe, J. Lumb, S. Firth.

General Committee — Officers and Messrs. N. Crowther, A. Smith, J. Sidda, A. Pearson, I. Holland, W. Core, S. Firth, G. Hamer, C. Sanderson and J. Stansfield.

Umpires — 1st Team—S. Core.
2nd Team—J. W. Fielding.

Captains — 1st Team—W. Nairn.
2nd Team—S. Pearson.

Vice-Captains — 1st Team—G. Hamer.
2nd Team—B. Hinchliffe.

---

# STONES METHODIST
# Cricket Club.

## FIXTURES FOR 1938

## and CRICKET CLUB RULES.

### Member's Card.

Name ...........................

J. MELLOR, PRINTER, RIPPONDEN.

---

## FIXTURES FOR 1938.
### FIRST ELEVEN.

| Date. | Name of Club. | Gr'nd. | Res'lt |
|---|---|---|---|
| Apl. 30 | Stainland | home | L |
| May 7 | Siddal | away | W |
| " 14 | Triangle | home | L |
| " 21 | Greetland | away | W |
| " 28 | 1st rd. Cup Barkisland | away | W |
| June 4 | Copley | home | W |
| W.M. 6 | Turnwrights & Clifton | home | |
| W.T. 7 | Sowerby | away | |
| June 11 | Mytholmroyd | home | |
| " 18 | Norwood Green | away | |
| " 25 | Stainland | home | |
| July 2 | Sowerby | home | |
| " 9 | Turnwrights & Clifton | away | |
| " 16 | | home | W |
| " 23 | Copley | home | L |
| " 30 | Siddal | | |
| Aug. 6 | Halifax Holidays. | | |
| " 13 | Halifax Holidays. | | |
| " 20 | Greetland | away | |
| " 27 | Mytholmroyd | home | |
| Sept. 3 | Norwood Green | away | |
| " 10 | Triangle | away | |

Ground — "Swift Cross," Ripponden.

---

### STONES
### METHODIST CRICKET CLUB.

#### RULES.

1.—That this Club be called the "Stones Methodist Cricket Club."

2.—That all business connected with the Club shall be left to the entire management of a Committee, consisting of the officers and ten members, all to be elected annually. Regular playing members not eligible to stand on the Selection Committee.

3.—That any member of the Committee being absent four consecutive meetings shall, unless he send an explanation which the Committee consider satisfactory, cease to be a member thereof. If necessary, the Committee shall be empowered to appoint a successor.

### HALIFAX CRICKET LEAGUE
#### 1971 FIXTURES

**Stones Junior XI (Section A)**

| Date | Opponents | Gr'd | Rslt |
|---|---|---|---|
| May 3 | Sowerby | A | |
| 10 | Barkisland | H | |
| 17 | Copley | A | |
| 24 | Blackley | H | |
| June 2 | Triangle | H | |
| 7 | Barkisland | A | |
| 14 | Copley | H | |
| 21 | S.B.C.I. | A | |
| 28 | Triangle | A | |
| July 5 | Sowerby | H | |
| Aug. 2/3 | Semi-Final: A Winners v C Winners | | |
| 9/10 | Final: Semi-Final Winners v B Winners | | |

John S. Crowther Printing Service, Ripponden

---

**STONES CRICKET CLUB**
**MEMBER'S CARD**
Officers for 1971

*President:* Mr H. Whitehead
*Honorary Vice-Presidents:* Messrs D. Booth, W. Gledhill, S. Pearson, H. Whiteley, R. Smith

*Hon. Subscribers:* Coun. J. W. Berry, Coun. G. Hayles, Messrs. J. Beverley, L. Barrett, J. B. Crawshaw, F. Crowther, G. Eastwood, G. Hamer, I. Holland, L. Holland, W. Marshall, C. Moores, W. Nairn, A. Smith, P. Smith, A. Spink, G. N. Turner, H. Taylor, G. Whiteley, H. Whiteley, P. H. Whiteley, J. Whiteley (i), J. Whiteley, H. Wolstenholme.

*Treasurer:* Mr H. Normanton
*Secretary:* Mr M. J. Brown, 1 Castle Estate, Ripponden
*Auditors:* Messrs G. Eastwood, R. Galloway

*Hon Subscription Collectors:* Messrs J. W. Whiteley, S. Palmer
*General Committee:* Messrs H. Heaton, A. Houlker, J. Kenworthy, B. Little, K. Jagger, A. Crawshaw, P. Party, F. Wilde, J. W. Whiteley
*Selection Committee:* Messrs M. J. Brown, J. W. Whiteley, F. Wilde, S. Palmer, H. Normanton
*1st XI Captain:* B. Little
*Vice-Captain:* A. Houlker
*2nd XI Captain:* J. D. Kenworthy
*Vice-Captain:* G. Habergham

---

### HALIFAX CRICKET LEAGUE
#### 1971 FIXTURES
**Stones Cricket Club 1st XI**
*Practice Nights: Tuesday and Thursday*
*Committee Meeting: 3rd Thursday each month*

| Date | Opponents | Gr'd | Rslt |
|---|---|---|---|
| May 1 | S.B.C.I. | A | |
| 8 | Sowerby | H | |
| 15 | Bradshaw | A | |
| 16 | Siddal (Cup) | H | |
| 22 | Stainland | H | |
| 23 | 2nd Round Cup | | |
| 29 | Triangle | A | |
| 31 | Triangle | H | |
| June 5 | Old Town | A | |
| 6 | Third Round Cup | | |
| 12 | Siddal | H | |
| 19 | Webster's | A | |
| 20 | Semi-Finals Cup | | |
| 26 | Mytholmroyd | H | |
| July 3 | Sowerby | A | |
| 24 | S.B.C.I. | H | |
| 31 | Bradshaw | H | |
| Aug. 7 | Stainland | A | |
| 14 | Old Town | H | |
| 21 | Siddal | A | |
| 28 | Webster's | H | |
| Sept. 4 | Mytholmroyd | A | |

---

**Stones Cricket Club**

#### RULES

1. That this Club be called the "Stones Cricket Club".

2. That all business connected with the Club shall be left to the entire management of a Committee, consisting of the officers and ten members, all to be elected annually. Regular playing members not eligible to stand on the Selection Committee.

3. That any member of the Committee being absent four consecutive meetings, shall, unless he send an explanation which the Committee consider satisfactory, cease to be a member thereof. If necessary, the Committee shall be empowered to appoint a successor.

4. That five shall constitute a quorum of the Committee, and twenty a quorum of the Club.

5. The Committee shall elect its own Chairman, who shall see that the business is conducted with regularity and dispatch, and in addition to one vote as a member of the Committee he shall have a casting vote.

## THORNTON CRICKET CLUB

A new chapter for Thornton Cricket Club began when their application to join Halifax Cricket League was accepted for the 2003 season.

They left the Bradford Central League as Waddilove Cup winners (1st team cup) and League runners-up to Buttershaw S.P. whom they had beaten in the cup final. Buttershaw went on to join the Central Yorkshire League and Thornton the Halifax Cricket League with great expectations from the previous season.

Those expectations were met, with John Ashley leading the side, the 1st XI won, the then Second Division of the League with a record number of points. Unfortunately the 2nd XI could not match them and they did not achieve promotion until the following year led by Peter Butterfield, when they won the Terry Wynne Conference.

Unfortunately, the success of the First team did not continue, most of the team had been together through the success of the nineties and gradually the team began to break apart. John Ashley resigned as captain during the 2004 season when the team finished 10th, just above the relegation places. The following two years 2005 and 2006 they managed to keep their Premier Division status, finishing 8th and 6th respectively, but the writing had been on the wall and in 2007 they were relegated.

Under new captain Greg Soames they re-grouped in the Roy Smith Conference and with an influx of young players brought through the Club's junior section they finished 4th in 2008 and in 2009 came 2nd and with it promotion back to the Premier Division. Momentum is key in sport and in 2010 the 1st team finished 4th and then 3rd in 2011. With the likes of Ross Soames who won the wicketkeeping trophy two years on the bounce, Ben Harris who won the bowling averages in 2012 and young Josh Hutchinson who was the county Joe Lumb player of the year, the future of the team looks bright and the decision to join the Halifax Cricket League vindicated.

## TRIANGLE CRICKET CLUB

*Commemorating and Celebrating Triangle Cricket Club's 150th Anniversary*

We can safely say that no one is still with us when Triangle Cricket Club was founded in 1862, which is a great pity because early accounts of the club are sparse and dates of events are sometimes conflicting. This is not unique to Triangle.

The men of 1862 and the following years were not interested in history. They wanted to play cricket. These are not dusty sheets of paper but the story of cricket at Grassy Bottoms.

How many other clubs can boast a 150th anniversary? It is known that cricket was played in Triangle long before this, and there are many legends about the village cricketers playing the game in a manly fashion on Norland Moor below the Ladstone.

Legend must not be too readily set aside though, as although the passage of time and the repetition of legends by successive generations by word of mouth often changes the detail, the basic facts are generally found to be true. The fields have a beautiful situation on the banks of the Ryburn stream, being surrounded by trees, and well away from the bustle of traffic on the main road.

Apart from cricket, the grounds have been used for local gatherings, ranging from sports meetings of many kinds to pop concerts and the Rushbearing, and it has always been valuable as a place where the inhabitants can find rest and relaxation on summer days, when it is a real suntrap.

Many of the local cricketers were, in their earliest days, taken down to the ground by their parents, and so their earliest acquaintance with Grassy Bottoms was made before they were in a position to realise anything about cricket.

## WARLEY CRICKET CLUB

Paradise Lane. Without doubt, the ideal name for a cricket ground.

Warley, who left the Amateur League for the Halifax League in 1953, have played at Paradise Lane continuously since 1933, and also before that as well. The club folded in 1919, only to re-emerge 14 years later. In the 1920's, when the club was temporarily defunct, cricket was still played at the ground.

Local history expert David Brearley says: 'Warley is now recognised as one of Calderdale's most attractive and unspoilt villages. It retains a semi-rural atmosphere and a charm which fortunately the residents will fight to keep.'

In years gone by, Warley was a township bordered to the west by Midgley and to the east by Ovenden. Today, many local folk still talk of Warley Town. Warley - or Werlafeslei, as it was known in the Domesday Book of 1086 - made its name as a farming area.

Today, it is famous for the Maypole Inn, the real hub of village life.

Warley's tree-lined ground is not a million miles away from that of Sowerby Bridge Church Institute CC.

Halifax Vandals rugby team is also based only a few hundred yards away.

As to the ground itself, it is immediately surrounded by houses, cottages, a church, a school and a children's playground, and as such, has a nice enclosed feel to it. The trees on the boundary's edge add to the pleasant ambience, and one or two actually over-hang the playing surface.

No-one could say that the outfield is totally flat, but over the years the club has made strenuous attempts to level out the lumps that, on occasions, have diverted balls skywards.

The ground is rented on an annual basis from a local family.

Paradise Lane has seen its fair share of improvements. The original pavilion had a new floor and new roof put in, and the current construction was built by club member Howard Smith in the 1960's.

Club stalwart Ian Buckley explains: 'Howard built the pavilion at home - literally. Other members helped him put it up and concrete the base, and overall it cost us £2,500. It would have cost double the amount if we had not done it ourselves.'

The old scorebox was also replaced, and a new tearoom has been added.

Triangle Cricket Club

J.W.Hall

2nd XI

Inserts: D.Oakes & E.Pullen  A.Whitehead  G.Hitchen  D.Hardy

H.Sunderland  J.Turner  K.Wilson  J.Parkin  K.Whalley  S.Andrews  E.Nicholl

A.G.M.Hall

1st XI

T.Madden  J.Clegg  G.Bruce  P.Ingham

N.Ashcroft  R.Rodger  G.Horsman  B.Hunter  G.Wood  B.Gamon  J.Pearcis

J.Rodger

Both Teams Winners of

2nd Div. Championship 1963

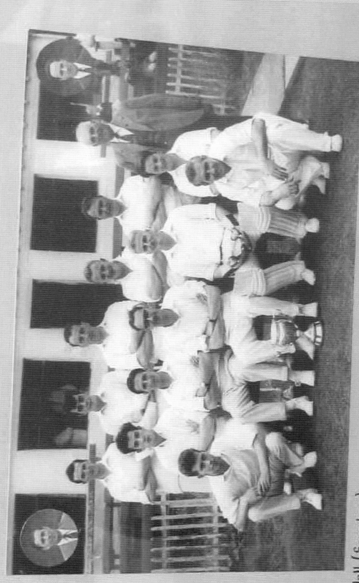

Triangle Cricket Club

1st. XI

J.W.Hall (Secretary)                                      A.G.M.Hall (President)
Back Row:- B.Normanton  D.Ackroyd  K.Wilson  B.Gannon  K.Senior  J.Rodger (Scorer)
Front Row:- B.Hunter  J.Clegg  G.Bruce  N.Ashcroft (Capt.) J.Patrick  G.Horsman  R.Rodger

Winners of  Halifax Cricket League
1st. Division Championship - 1964

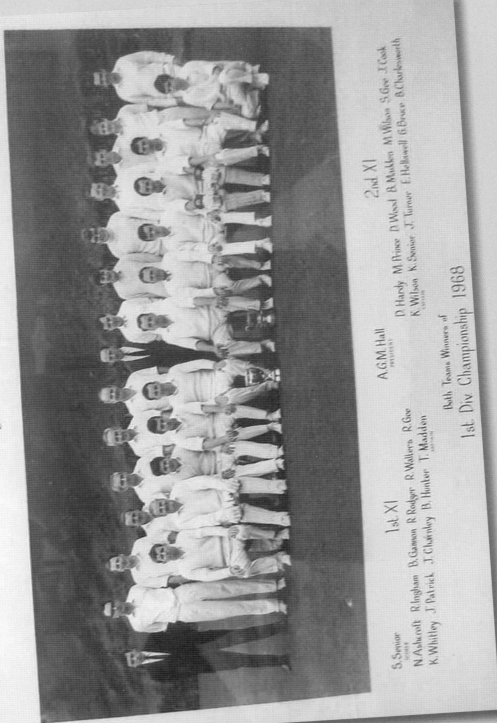

Triangle Cricket Club

1st XI

S. Senior
SCORER

N. Ashcroft   R. Ingham   B. Gannon   R. Rodger   R. Walters   R. Gee
K. Whitley   J. Patrick   J. Charnley   B. Hunter   T. Madden
CAPTAIN

A.G.M. Hall
PRESIDENT

2nd XI

D. Hardy   M. Prince   D. Wood   B. Madden   M. Wilson   S. Gee   J. Cook
R. Wilson   K. Senior   J. Turner   E. Hollowell   G. Bruce   B. Charlesworth
CAPTAIN

Both Teams Winners of

1st. Div Championship 1968

Triangle Cricket Club

S. Senior
SCORER

1st. XI

A.G.M. Hall
PRESIDENT

2nd. XI

N.Ashcroft  R.Ingham  B.Gannon  R.Rodger  R.Walters  R.Gee      D.Hardy  M.Prince  D.Wood  B.Madden  M.Wilson  S.Gee  J.Cook
K.Whitley  J.Patrick  J.Charnley  B.Hunter  T.Madden            K.Wilson  K.Senior  J.Turner  E.Hellawell  G.Bruce  B.Charlesworth
          (CAPTAIN)                                                      (CAPTAIN)

Both Teams Winners of

1st. Div. Championship 1969

Buckley, who as a boy during the war acted as club scorer, played for Warley for several decades, and has been a Committee member since 1957. He has vivid memories: 'In the early days we had a problem with the grass. It was too long. Sometimes you could run five for a gentle push! In the end we had to move some sheep in to graze during the week - just so it would be short enough for the weekend. Nowadays we have got a good cricket wicket, but it has been a long process. Decades ago, balls would fly off a length, but we added some clay to the wicket and then it began to be a very good track to bat on.'

The pitch was obviously kind to Warley in the 1990's. They won the Parish Cup in 1990, 1992, 1996 and 2001, and the First Division Championship in 1998.

## WIBSEY PARK CHAPEL CRICKET CLUB

The club was formed in 1887 and joined the Bradford Mutual Sunday School League in 1908 where it played until 1998. At that time it was the oldest surviving member of the League, only missing one season since joining.

Originally club members were drawn from the membership of Park Methodist Church in West Bowling, Bradford, and although that is not the case today, the club still retains links with the church through a number of both playing and non playing members.

The club had a proud record in the Sunday School League, having been League championship winners on no less that sixteen occasions and playing in the top division of the League most of the time.

In 1999 the club modified its name to reflect the area in which it now plays and draws most of its membership from. At the same time, it was accepted in to the Bradford Central Cricket League where its two main teams played, as well as retaining a third team in the Mutual Sunday School League. In 2000 links were finally severed with the Sunday School League, when it had two more teams accepted in the Dales Council League. In 2005 the club voted on going back to three teams. This was accepted due to the lack of quality senior players in the lower teams.

Today the club can boast some 100 active members, drawn from all walks of life and ethnic backgrounds, in accordance with the equal opportunities policy in its membership. Four senior teams play each week during the summer, as well as a midweek evening team and four junior teams at Under 13, 15 and 17 levels. The club takes development of junior cricketers very seriously, filling the gap in the provision of facilities for the local community, as well as the void left by the demise of sporting activities at school. Additionally, it provides a continuous pool of players to help maintain the traditions and future of the club.

To support so much cricketing activity the club operates from two grounds – its home base at Haycliffe Lane, adjoining the special school, and the former Yorkshire County Cricket ground at Park Avenue, which it hopes will provide the infrastructure for continually improving and raising the quality and standard of cricket in the future.

The club joined the Halifax Cricket League in 2009 from the Bradford Central League.

# Ex-Clubs

## Halifax Parish Cricket League 1914 to 1925
### and then
## Halifax Cricket League from 1926 onwards
### *Former member clubs in order of leaving the league*

**Compiled from an extract from:**
**Lost: The Former Cricket Clubs and Cricket Grounds of Halifax and Calderdale by Andrew Hardcastle (Cricket Heritage publications 2006) and updated by David Normanton, all accomplished with permission from Andrew Hardcastle (2014).**

### Lightcliffe (1914)

Lightcliffe were one of the founding members of the Halifax & District League in 1894 and became one of the founding members of the Halifax Parish League. They played just the one season before moving to the Spen Valley League temporarily due to the Great War. The club re-established their association with the League when they joined the Sunday League in 2001.

### Clifton Britannia (1914-15 and 1924-36)

This club had been playing since at least 1870 on a field behind the Armytage Arms at Clifton, becoming members in the Brighouse League, then the Halifax and District League before becoming founder members of the Parish League. Like Siddal they too joined the Halifax section of the Yorkshire Council in 1916 but stayed there one year longer until 1923,They reverted to the Parish League in 1924 winning the title in1925. They remained loyal to the League until 1936 but after that season ended they were given notice to quit their ground by the landlord, who allocated it to Blakeborough's Sports Association. The club did not immediately disband remaining dormant pending a revival chance. They amalgamated with Turner & Wainwright's to play at Brookfoot as Turnwrights & Clifton from 1937 to 1939.

### Siddal (1914-15,1922-39 and 1949-94)

Began life as Siddal St Marks Young Men around 1879, their first League cricket being played in the Halifax Amateur League and the District League. They bought their own ground in 1902 at Park Lane for £450, the money being subscribed by members in the form of shares, adding a brick pavilion in 1903 and became the instigators of the Parish League. A highly regarded club, they were invited to join a Halifax Section of the Yorkshire Council in 1916 playing there until 1921 when they rejoined, and again in 1940 to 1948 were members of the Yorkshire Council. They won the title in 1936 and the Parish Cup in 1912, 1928 and 1937. Their third stint saw them rejoin in 1949 staying on until 1994. The club fell on hard times in the 1990's and were forced to resign after the 1994 season through lack of playing numbers, the ground was taken over by Halifax Association club West End.

## Elland Edge (1914 - 1916)

This club was a former Halifax and District League and Amateur League Club who were not originally chosen as founder members of the Parish League. They took the place of Ovenden who became defunct over a ground issue after season 1913 ended. It seemed that the team would fold before the 1916 season started due to the War but they continued on for one last year.

## Illingworth St Mary's (1914-1919 and 1942)

Illingworth St. Mary's CC joined the Ovenden & District League in 1896 and thus crossed swords with Mountain United, Bradshaw Mills, Lee Mount Baptists, Ovenden St. George's and Ovenden Albion, and went on to play in the Halifax Parish League as founding members and then to the Yorkshire Council. With the Halifax League suspended due to war, fixtures were arranged with Yorkshire Cricket Council clubs and they rejoined the Halifax Parish League. They were champions in 1916 and 1919. The club postponed an application to the new Halifax section of the Yorkshire Cricket Council in 1915 because of the war. In 1917 it decided to arrange fixtures against the Council's members, in order 'to keep the club going'. The continuation of cricket, competitive if possible, was not regarded as unpatriotic in order to comply with Yorkshire Cricket Council requirements, the facilities at the Coach House were improved, at a cost of £200, and an away dressing room added. The club played one more year in 1942 during the Second World War. The club renewed their membership joining the Sunday League in 2001.

## Siddal United (1919)

This club was a former member of the Amateur League, with a high quality ground in Park Lane. This ground was located just below that of Siddal. Unfortunately for them it was used by Halifax Town A.F.C. and the overlapping seasons created problems with pitch preparation. United were never able to use their own ground in the Parish League, playing all their matches away from home in their one season in the League and suspended operations in 1920.

## Norland (1921)

This is another former Amateur League club who were elected despite not being particularly successful. They were rejected in 1920 for their ground being very difficult to get to. They played on a field in the village opposite to the entrance to the golf course. They inevitably struggled in this higher grade of cricket and finished bottom of the League. In 1922 they moved to the Halifax and District League.

## Northowram (1921-1922)

Northowram St Matthew's CC was formed in 1907 and the club was linked to the parish church and as such were occasionally referred to as Northowram Parish Church CC. The club originally played at Shibden Park before playing on two other grounds. In 1920 they moved to their current ground at Westercroft Lane. In 1919 the club became members of The Halifax & District Cricket League. It is probable that the club were admitted to the Parish League in 1921 because of their new ground. It is interesting to note that the Parish League referred only to them as Northowram CC. They played in the League two years before joining the newly amalgamated Halifax & District Amateur League in 1923. Northowram came back to the Halifax League Sunday section for two seasons again in 1994 and 1995. We currently know this club as Northowram Fields and they have now played in our Sunday League since 2010.

## Halifax Baptists (1919 – 1922)

This club was elected following successful seasons in the Halifax Amateur League. They had a ground at Nursery Lane, Ovenden. They fared reasonably well, finishing as high as fourth in 1921. In 1923 they joined the newly formed Halifax Association where they remained until 1940.

## Elland A (1921-1923)

Elland's 1st XI at that time played in the Yorkshire Cricket Council which in 1921, had ended the Group system. A copy of the league table at May 21 1921 shows Elland A at the top of the first team division. It is probable that travel costs were one of the reasons that their 2nd XI played in the Parish League for these 3 years. In 1926 the club moved to the Huddersfield and District League and have remained there ever since although it is now called the Huddersfield Drakes League. Elland renewed their ties with Halifax League when they entered a side in the Sunday League in 2006.

## Smith Bulmer's (1929 – 1930)

Halifax Association Champions in 1927 and 1928 but the textile workers found life more difficult in their new sphere. They finished bottom in 1930 and this led to their demise.
Their ground was on Beechwood Avenue, Holmfield.

## Halifax B (1930 – 1934 and 1940)

Initially the third team of Yorkshire Council side Halifax, enjoying one of their more successful periods at this time, with Heath Old Boys taking their 2nd XI fixtures. From 1932 it was Halifax 2nd XI who played as Halifax and won the League both in 1932 and 1933.

## Heath Old Boys (1930 - 34)

This was a cricket section from the Rugby Union Club who formed this team of the same name. They never operated in the 1st XI's league but took the 2nd XI fixtures initially of Halifax "B" then Turner & Wainwright's playing in this latter period at Brookfoot. After finishing bottom on 1934 they did not reappear with their place being taken by Blakeborough's. An earlier Heath Old Boys team had played a season in the Halifax & District League.

## Turner & Wainwright's (1922 – 1936)
## then Turnwright's & Clifton (1937-1939)

This club was formed in 1920 playing two seasons in the Amateur League with employees only. On election to the Parish League membership was thrown open to outsiders and the Parish Cup was won in 1925 together with the League Championship but by the 1930's there were problems with numbers. In 1933 and 1934 their 2nd XI fixtures were fulfilled by Heath Old Boys and in 1935 & 1936 by Blakeborough's. When Blakeborough's went alone on Clifton's old ground, it was expedient to amalgamate with the otherwise defunct Clifton to become Turnwright's & Clifton for the 3 years 1937 – 1939. When war broke out in 1939 the pleasantly situated ground by the canal at Brookfoot was ploughed up and was later largely covered by industrial premises.

## Norwood Green (1914-40)

This club began in the Halifax Amateur Cricket League in 1906 at a ground described as Wyke but April 1907 saw the opening of a new ground at Upper Rooke Farm. They won the League play-offs in 1906 and moved to the Halifax and District League for season 1908 remaining there until 1913. In 1914 they became one of the founding members of the Parish League and remained until 1940 folding soon after the outbreak of the Second World War. They were League Champions in 1921. Their ground was taken over for a time by the Craven Gentlemen. It was not until 1974 that the club emerged with this original name and played in the Bradford Central League.

## Blakeborough's Sports Association
## (1939 -1942, 1944 – 1946 and 1951–1956)

After taking the 2nd XI fixtures of Turner & Wainwright's in 1935 and 1936 they went alone in 1937 joining the Huddersfield and District Cricket Association after poaching Clifton's Armytage Arms ground by negotiation with the landlord. Their move to the Halifax League in 1939 was seen as a step up but an even bigger step up was achieved in 1947 when they switched to the Central Yorkshire Section of the Yorkshire Council League. In 1948 they found themselves without a groundsman and had to withdraw their entry in 1948 becoming temporarily defunct but they were back in business in 1950 joining the Huddersfield Association and were welcomed back into the Halifax League in 1951.They remained in the League until 1956 withdrawing for a final time at the end of this season. Their grounds at Clifton being left to decay until houses were eventually built on the site.

## Army XI (1944-1945)

A team formed from soldiers based at the Wellesley Park Barracks during the Second World War. They had a couple of successful seasons being well placed in the final tables but ceased to exist when the War ended.

## 3-Redep (1945)

Another war-time side representing The Royal Engineers Depot who had played in the Halifax Association since 1942, winning the Collinson Cup in 1944 and the League probably as well, though no final table survives. They actually played on Copley's ground. Copley ceased playing during the 1941-45 period retaining membership by paying their vice-president subs.

## King Cross (1952 – 1960 and 2004 – 2010)

They started out in 1878 as King Cross Wesleyans and won the Parish Cup for the first time in 1892. The Parish Cup was won for a fifth time in 1916 when our League was only 3 seasons old. They joined the Yorkshire Council League in 1906 and played at The Ramsdens, which was named after the family who helped purchase it, after first playing at Savile Park and then renting a ground at West View. A further 4 Parish Cup wins were achieved before they joined our League for the first time. For economic reasons the club did not engage a professional in 1952 and switched to the Halifax League joining at the same time as Mytholmroyd Methodists. The club remained until the 1960 season and joined the Central Yorkshire League Section of the Yorkshire Council in1961. They rejoined in 2004 being promoted in 2005 as Conference

Champions but finished bottom of the Premier Division in 2006. In 2009 the club finished bottom of the first division being relegated to the second division and at the end of 2010 season the seconds were also relegated to the second division. Their Sunday Section side had withdrawn at the end of the 2009 season. The painful decision to end the cricket club's 133 year existence was taken at an emergency meeting held on Sunday 6 February 2011 at the clubhouse. Club stalwart Richard Pinder described the demise as extremely sad for all involved but a lack of volunteers to work behind the scenes combined with an ageing squad were the main reasons behind the sudden but not lightly taken decision.

## Salem, Hebden Bridge (1954 – 1962)

This club had previously played their cricket in the Hebden Bridge League having earlier featured in the Calder Valley League and Sowerby Division League. They had never been particularly successful but had a very small picturesque ground at Hollins Holme. They were one of the four teams added in 1954, along with Blackley, Bradshaw and Warley, to allow the League to expand to two divisions. They remained a division two side and switched to the Halifax Amateur Association in 1963 and later changed their name to Hebden Bridge.

## Webster's (1951 – 1978)

Brewery based side who had played in the Halifax Association since 1926 at first they played on a sloping field in Ovenden Wood Road before moving to Cross Roads at Wainstalls in 1935. They had been Association Champions in 1950 and won the Parish Cup in 1956 but by 1978 they were in difficulties and after finishing bottom of division two resigned just before the start of the 1979 season. A feature of the League Handbook was Webster's Brewery advert which ran from 1951 to 1994 and appeared on the back cover from 1974.

## Dean Clough/Crossley's Carpets from 1963 (1939 – 1980)

They took their place in our League after becoming the 1938 champions of the Halifax Association where they had played since 1932. Their ground was located at Ovenden on the Mason Green Ground. This was another famous name to grace our League when in 1963 they changed their name from the one associated with the mill complex to the name of the company running the complex and that name was Crossley's Carpets. In 1970 the Parish Cup was won and at the time of their demise they were a competent first division side. The company became part of the Kidderminster based Carpet's International and closed the Dean Clough site in 1982.

## R.A.F.A. (1983 – 1988)

The Royal Air Force Association side were long serving members of The Halifax Association from 1952 to 1982. The club had improved their profile by moving to a large new ground at Old Earth, Elland in 1981. The move came about because a number of their players had connections with the soccer team that played at the same location. This move ultimately led to them being accepted into the Halifax League in 1983. Playing success was rare, the team being wooden spoonists in 1983, 1984 and 1988. They were replaced for the 1989 season by Southowram and subsequently folded.

## Mackintosh's (1962 -1995)

This club was formed in 1960 as Mackintosh's Saturday CC. This club was the third famous national name to feature in our League. They originally played in the Halifax Association but were quickly admitted to the Halifax League in 1962 due to their very fine ground situated at West Vale. The club enjoyed some success winning the second division championship in 1981. In May 1995 the League asked the club to clarify its future and it was stated that its ground would be available to them for all of 1995 but the situation would be reviewed at the end of the season. Subsequently at the end of the season they lost their ground when it was sold by the then owners Nestle. This was a very unfortunate situation for some players who had joined that year from the defunct Siddal club and now found themselves without a club again. One notable claim to fame that occurred on the ground was that an England Cricket Captain's reign ended on their grounds. I quote "My eleven year reign as England cricket captain ended abruptly on a Sunday afternoon in mid July 1977. Fittingly the sun did not shine that day: it was damp, dark and drizzling and as I walked across the cricket pitch in Halifax it seemed as if I was walking to the gallows; my stomach felt empty and I was strangely nervous." This is the opening paragraph of Rachel Heyhoe Flints autobiography and the event took place at Mackintosh's Cricket Club.

## Barkisland (1939 – 2000)

The club was formed in 1899 and played in the Halifax Amateur Cricket League, moving to the Halifax & District League in 1921 before being part of the amalgamated Halifax & District Amateur Cricket Association in 1923. They remained in that League until 1938 being accepted into the Halifax League in 1939 and shortly afterwards in the early war years won the League in 1941 before claiming it again three times in four years between 1947 and 1950, and yet again in 1955 and 1956. In 1957 there were three pairs of brothers in the Barkisland team namely the Schofields, the Hallowells and the Tennysons. It would be 1975 before they won it again but what a year that was when the Australian cricket legend Dennis Lillee opened their new pavilion in the same year. Our past League Chairman Barry Tennyson was a very successful Captain bringing the championship back on three occasions in 1977, 1984 & 1985, doing the double in 1977 by winning the Parish Cup also. The club celebrated its centenary in 1999 and in 2000 took the decision to leave the Halifax League switching to the Huddersfield League in 2001.

## Salendine Nook Old Boys (1998 – 2004)

SNOB's as they were known, were a Huddersfield based side who had figured in the Huddersfield Central League and Huddersfield Association. They were formed in 1975 at Salendine Nook High School. After a promising seventh place finish in their debut season in 1998 SNOB's became regular re-election applicants. After only seven seasons in the League the club took the decision in February 2005 to quit due to a shortage of players and repeated vandalism at the club.

## Mytholmroyd Methodist's/Halifax from 2005 (1952 – 2008)

This club began their cricketing journey in 1894 as Mytholmroyd Wesleyan Sunday School CC playing first in the Calder Valley League and then moving to the Hebden Bridge League the following year. In 1906 they moved to The Holmes on Scout Road in Mytholmroyd remaining here until 2004. In 1933 they changed their name to Mytholmroyd Methodist's. During the Second World War the Hebden Bridge League was suspended so they joined the Halifax &

District Amateur League and made the switch to the Halifax League in 1952. It seems to be that when something major occurred historically then something special happened to Mytholmroyd Methodist's. In 1963 when Kennedy was assassinated then a new pavilion was erected. It was the Primary Department Room at Mount Zion Primitive Methodist Church in Mytholmroyd and was brought over to the ground when both Methodist churches in the village joined together. In 1969 when man landed on the moon Meths first XI were the Division 2 Champions and when Margaret Thatcher became Prime Minister in 1979 then the 2nd XI won the Division 2 Championship. In 1983 when the seat belt law was introduced and Breakfast TV commenced then the 2nd XI achieved the same feat again as in 1979, this was to be the last piece of silverware for the club. In 2004 they suffered a fire which destroyed their wooden tea hut. In the early hours of Saturday morning 25th September, 2004 the wooden structure blazed for three hours as retained firemen tackled the blaze. In addition local people had been campaigning to keep the cricket ground on Scout Road following suggestions that the land was to be sold by the church. In November 2004 the club announced that it was merging with Halifax Cricket Club continuing to play at Scout Road in 2005 before moving to a new ground at Exley in 2006. This positive move was thought to be a future securing move for both clubs at that time , however in April 2009 the relatively newly merged club was forced to quit the League in the week before they were due to play Queensbury in the opening fixture. The problem arose with a loss of key players in the close season followed by a large number of transfer requests leading up to the start, which left the club with only 15 players.

## Augustinians (1997 – 2013)

Augustinians CC emerged in the late 1960's. One irreverent note often quoted was that the club was formed 'from the remnants of John Finbar Harold's darts team', but the reality was that the new side was connected to St. Augustine's Voluntary School, Bradley Bar. According to the official history of the Huddersfield Association:  It was at the November meeting in 1967 that "Mr Grimes, representing the staff, students, former students and friends of St. Augustine's Voluntary School, expressed his club's hopes of being admitted to the Association in 1968 and replied to questions put to him by various representatives." The representatives of the school were indeed successful and 1968 turned out to be Augustinians' debut season in the Association. When St. Augustine's merged with a nearby school, St. Gregory's Grammar, in the late-1970s to form All Saints School, the cricket club continued to thrive, recruiting staff, pupils and old boys from all three institutions.

In the early days, the club was indebted to a number of key individuals: Brian Doran, Frank Heppenstall, Peter Lawrence-Brown and Vincent O'Hara, plus Harold Ainley (1st XI captain) and Stuart Burns (2nd XI skipper) and then there was John Harold a stalwart of the side in its infancy. Harold also served as President of the Association. His term of office began in 1975 and he was in post in 1986 when the League celebrated its centenary.

Augustinians had their fair share of success. The 2nd XI won the Crosland Trophy in 1973, retained it the year after, and won it again in 1985. Meanwhile, the 1st XI claimed the Section A title four years out of five in the early 1980s, and won the Lumb Cup in 1984 to boot. Not surprisingly, they were dubbed the 'team of the eighties'.

If this was the up side, the down side was one particular encounter with Almondbury Wesleyans. The club scorebook shows that the eleven men representing Augustinians were dismissed for a combined total of six with byes top-scoring with two. As if to put such disasters into context, a spokesman said: 'The club, and the friendships it has fostered over the years, survived such setbacks and, hopefully, even if the circle were once more to turn, they would continue for many years to come.'

Augustinians CC used to play at All Saints School, but were restricted in what they could do with the cricket field during the week because it was part of the School's premises. They made the move to Laund Hill at the beginning of the 1990s. One of the most significant events in the history of Augustinians Cricket Club was the move out of the Huddersfield Association into the higher profile and well respected Halifax League. Both John Harold and Harold Ainley described it as "the biggest change" during their careers "along with the ground move to Laund Hill."

John Harold said of Augustinians' move from the Huddersfield Association to the Halifax League: "We decided on the move because we weren't going anywhere in the Huddersfield Association and the club needed a change in order to progress. It has turned out to be the right move because we are playing cricket of a better standard and have gained more exposure.

Augustinians had a number of issues that had caused genuine concern over the past few years to the club. Their 17 season stay in the Halifax League ended after it was confirmed that they would not be allowed to apply for re-election at the November 2013 Annual General Meeting.

They have unfortunately lost their ground at the Huddersfield YMCA complex at Laund Hill and have been unable to find a suitable alternative for next season before the end of September 2013 deadline. The club made a late bid to use the former Halifax CC ground at Park Lane School but that attempt failed as there were issues over the lease of the Exley pitch and Halifax League Chiefs had ruled that it would not be of sufficient standard anyway having not been used for cricket since 2009.

Well what about Laund Hill? What were its defining characteristics as a cricketing arena? Martin Farrar's view is that "The imposing ring of trees that circled the playing area. I'm a spin bowler, and on a dark afternoon I like to give the ball a bit of flight, so it comes out of the trees and deceives the batsman. The trees are definitely a big help to bowlers!"

# Ex-Clubs: Pictures

## A selection images from former Halifax League clubs

*Augustinians*

It all augurs well for Augustinians — the All Saints side made the trip to Badger Hill on Saturday and returned with three points. Back row (from left): C Ainley, T Lomax, J Wedge, C Walton, P Walton, P Hepworth. Front row: W Cratchley, H Ainley, C Charles, A Fearnley, J Harold

*Barkisland*

## Clifton.

A great revival of interest has been created during the winter in connection with the Clifton cricket club, and an optimistic feeling exists with respect to the season commencing to-morrow. No new players have yet joined, but a strong side under the captaincy of Harold Stead will be fielded, as he has the promise of support of Albert Sugden, and the Clifton stalwarts (S. White and J. Firth), besides several promising youngsters. Although the batting and bowling is likely to be weakened by the loss of Alfred Robinson, who has joined the Baildon Green club in the Bradford League, no season has yet passed without one youngster or another making his mark, so there are hopeful prospects. The club would welcome the services of a good wicket keeper. The second team will be captained by Geo. A. Stillingfleet, whose experience and judgment should prove an asset in developing the junior talent. The club will again play in the Halifax League and the Brighouse and District Evening League, and the committee are also co-operating with the Juvenile Organisation Committee.

April 26—Stainland ............................... away
May 3—Halifax ................................... home
  „  10—Sowerby .................................. away
  „  17—Copley ................................... home
  „  24—Smith Bulmers ............................ home
  „  31—First Round Cup
June 7—Triangle ................................. away
  „  9—(W.M.) Norwood Green ...................... home
  „  10—(W.T.) Mytholmroyd ....................... away
  „  14—Siddal ................................... home
  „  17 and 18—Turner and Wain ................... home
  „  21—Greetland ................................ away
  „  28—Stainland ................................ home
July 1 and 2—Norwood Green ...................... away
  „  5—Smith Bulmers ............................. away
  „  12—Copley ................................... away
  „  19—Greetland ................................ home
  „  26—Sowerby .................................. home
Aug. 2—Turner and Wain .......................... away
  „  9—Mytholmroyd ............................... home
  „  16—Wakes Holiday.
  „  23—Halifax .................................. away
  „  30—Triangle ................................. home
Sept. 6—Siddal .................................. away

Second teams vice-versa with the exception of the Halifax dates when the Juniors meet Heath Old Boys.

*Clifton Britannia*

### Clifton Britannia Cricket Club.
WINNERS OF THE HALIFAX PARISH LEAGUE.
Season 1925.

*Clifton*

*Elland A League Table*

# Sport and Pastime.

## HALIFAX PARISH CRICKET LEAGUE

League table up to May 21:—

### First Teams.

|  | P. | W. | L. | D. | Pts. |
|---|---|---|---|---|---|
| Elland A | 8 | 4 | 1 | 1 | 9 |
| Greetland | 5 | 3 | 0 | 2 | 8 |
| Norwood Green | 5 | 4 | 1 | 0 | 8 |
| Mytholmroyd | 5 | 3 | 2 | 0 | 6 |
| Norland | 5 | 2 | 2 | 0 | 6 |
| Baptists | 5 | 2 | 2 | 1 | 5 |
| Northowram | 6 | 2 | 3 | 1 | 5 |
| Triangle | 6 | 2 | 4 | 0 | 4 |
| Stainland | 6 | 1 | 4 | 1 | 3 |
| St. Peter's | 5 | 0 | 4 | 1 | 1 |

### Second Teams.

|  | P. | W. | L. | D. | Pts. |
|---|---|---|---|---|---|
| Greetland | 4 | 4 | 0 | 0 | 8 |
| Stainland | 5 | 4 | 1 | 0 | 8 |
| Norwood Green | 3 | 3 | 0 | 0 | 6 |
| Mytholmroyd | 4 | 3 | 1 | 0 | 6 |
| St. Peter's | 5 | 2 | 3 | 0 | 4 |
| Baptists | 4 | 1 | 2 | 1 | 3 |
| Northowram | 5 | 1 | 3 | 1 | 3 |
| Norland | 5 | 1 | 4 | 0 | 2 |
| Triangle | 5 | 0 | 5 | 0 | 0 |

Saturday's Results.—First Teams: Triangle 96, Stainland 82; Northowram 74, Norland 51; Baptists 19, Norwood Green 21 for 3; Elland A 247 for 8 (dec.), Greetland 194 for 7, Mytholmroyd 167, St. Peter's 129. Second Teams: Triangle 63, Stainland 64 for 8; Norland 52, Northowram 59 for 1, Mytholmroyd 91, St. Peter's 56.

Matches and Officials for Saturday.—First teams: Northowram v. Greetland; umpires, Elland A and Mytholmroyd. Second Teams: Greetland v. Northowram; Baptists and Mytholmroyd. Norwood Green v. Baptists; St. Peter's and

# HALIFAX CRICKET CLUB
### HALIFAX LEAGUE & HALIFAX PARISH CHALLENGE CUP WINNERS, 1932

*Halifax (1)*

*Halifax (2)*

*Illingworth CC*

KING CROSS CRICKET CLUB – 1882

# MYTHOLMROYD METHODISTS C.C.
## HX7

Mytholmroyd Methodists

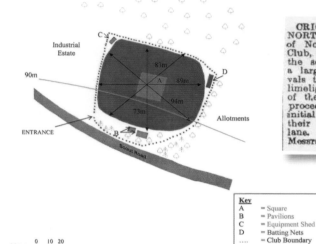

Industrial Estate

90m

ENTRANCE

Scout Road

Allotments

**Key**

| | |
|---|---|
| A | = Square |
| B | = Pavilions |
| C | = Equipment Shed |
| D | = Batting Nets |
| .... | = Club Boundary |
| ↔ | = Distance (metres) |
| ○ | = Trees |
| ⚘ | = Bushes |
| — | = Contour Line |

Metres  0  10  20
Foot  10  50

GEORGE CLAYTON – UNIVERSITY OF HUDDERSFIELD – 15/6/2004

CRICKET CLUB DANCE AT NORTHOWRAM.—Under the auspices of Northowram Parish Church Cricket Club, a successful dance was held in the schoolroom on Saturday, at which a large number assembled. At intervals the lights were turned low and limelight was thrown in various parts of the room with pleasing effect. The proceeds are to partly defray the initial cost of the laying of the crease at their new cricket ground in Westcroft-lane. The work has been done by Messrs. Conway, Halifax.

Northowram

Norwood Green

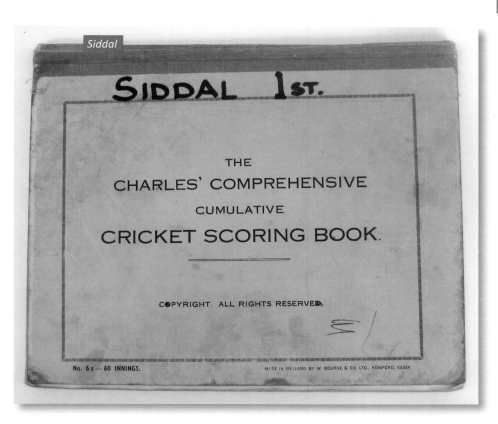

Siddal

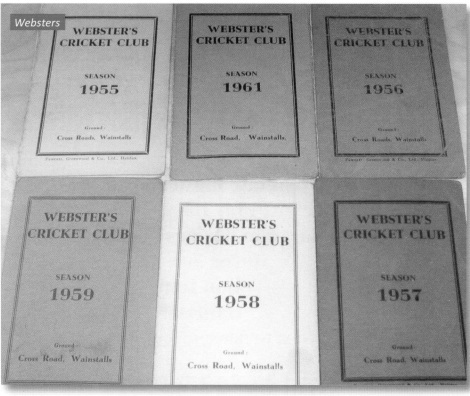

Websters

# YORKSHIRE

## TIMBER
## &
## BUILDERS
## MERCHANTS

## 01422 350073

www.yorkshiretimbermerchants.co.uk

*Proud Sponsors Of*

*Bridgeholme C.C.*

# Pictorial Tour of the Current Grounds

## Calder Valley Clubs

Booth

Bridgeholme

Luddendenfoot

Mytholmroyd

Old Town

Sowerby Bridge

Sowerby Bridge Church Institute

Sowerby St. Peter's

Warley

# M62 Corridor Clubs

Blackley

Greetland

Outlane

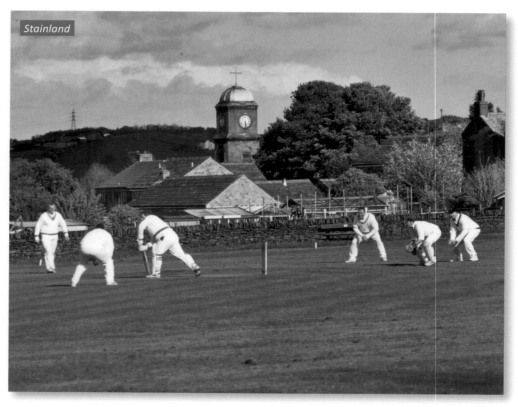

Stainland

Stones

Triangle

# Towards Bradford Clubs

Clayton

Cullingworth

Denholme Clough

Jer Lane

Low Moor

Oxenhope

Queensbury

Thornton

Wibsey Park Chapel

# Halifax Central Clubs

Bradshaw

Copley

Northowram Hedge Top

Old Crossleyans

Shelf

Southowram

# Halifax Cricket League Honours

## 1st DIVISION 1st TEAMS

| Year | Team | Player |
|------|------|--------|
| 1914 | Sowerby Bridge | |
| 1915 | Sowerby Bridge | |
| 1916 | Illingworth St Mary's | |
| 1917 | League Suspended – World War 1 | |
| 1918 | League Suspended – World War 1 | |
| 1919 | Illingworth St Mary's | |
| 1920 | Greetland | |
| 1921 | Norwood Green | |
| 1922 | Mytholmroyd | |
| 1923 | Triangle | |
| 1924 | Greetland | |
| 1925 | Clifton Britannia | |
| 1926 | Clifton Britannia | |
| 1927 | Triangle | |
| 1928 | Triangle | |
| 1929 | Greetland | |
| 1930 | Greetland | |
| 1931 | Triangle | |
| 1932 | Halifax 2nd XI | |
| 1933 | Halifax 2nd XI | |
| 1934 | Copley | |
| 1935 | Mytholmroyd | |
| 1936 | Siddal | |
| 1937 | Mytholmroyd | |
| 1938 | Stainland | |
| 1939 | Mytholmroyd | |
| 1940 | Mytholmroyd | |
| 1941 | Barkisland | |
| 1942 | Mytholmroyd | |
| 1943 | Mytholmroyd | B Bowe |
| 1944 | Mytholmroyd | |
| 1945 | Mytholmroyd | |
| 1946 | Greetland | W Normanton |
| 1947 | Barkisland | J Maude |
| 1948 | Mytholmroyd | H Ellis |
| 1949 | Barkisland | J Maude |
| 1950 | Barkisland | J Maude |
| 1951 | Copley | R Smith |
| 1952 | Copley | D Hardcastle |
| 1953 | Mytholmroyd | F K Smith |
| 1954 | Mytholmroyd | F K Smith |
| 1955 | Barkisland | J Maude |
| 1956 | Barkisland | J Maude |
| 1957 | Greetland | G S Hellowell |
| 1958 | Booth | F Wade |
| 1959 | Greetland | G S Hellowell |
| 1960 | Copley | J Farrar |
| 1961 | Greetland | N J Ellis |
| 1962 | Booth | D Livesey |
| 1963 | Sowerby St Peters | D Habergham |
| 1964 | Triangle | N Ashcroft |
| 1965 | Triangle | N Ashcroft |
| 1966 | Northowram | A Butterworth |
| 1967 | Booth | W Thomas |
| 1968 | Triangle | T Madden |
| 1969 | Triangle | J Patrick |
| 1970 | Greetland | G Scott |
| 1971 | Copley | B Hulme |
| 1972 | Triangle | J C Moncrief |
| 1973 | Copley | B Hulme |
| 1974 | Copley | B Hulme |
| 1975 | Barkisland | J Barron |
| 1976 | Copley | I Ball |
| 1977 | Barkisland | I S B Tennyson |
| 1978 | Warley | B Hulme |
| 1979 | Booth | R Collinge |
| 1980 | Barkisland | R J Davies |
| 1981 | Sowerby St Peters | S Casaru |
| 1982 | Triangle | J Parker |
| 1983 | Triangle | J Parker |
| 1984 | Barkisland | I S B Tennyson |
| 1985 | Barkisland | I S B Tennyson |
| 1986 | Warley | A Oates |
| 1987 | Booth | I Sharkey |
| 1988 | Copley | R Thorpe |
| 1989 | Copley | R Thorpe |
| 1990 | Booth | M Thomas |
| 1991 | Triangle | W Morris |
| 1992 | Bradshaw | C Sutcliffe |
| 1993 | Triangle | D Hudson |
| 1994 | Triangle | D Hudson |
| 1995 | Booth | T Conway |
| 1996 | Triangle | G Rodger |
| 1997 | Bradshaw | W Cotton |
| 1998 | Warley | A Oates |
| 1999 | Triangle | P Madden |
| 2000 | Copley | R Thorpe |
| 2001 | Copley | R Thorpe |
| 2002 | Booth | W Ali |
| 2003 | Copley | R Thorpe |

## CHANGE IN FORMAT TO A PREMIER DIVISION AND TWO FIRST DIVISION CONFERENCES
## PREMIER 1st TEAMS

| | | |
|---|---|---|
| 2004 | Copley | C Goulden |
| 2005 | Warley | M Midwood |
| 2006 | Bradshaw | W Cotton |
| 2007 | Mytholmroyd | K Halstead |
| 2008 | Warley | M Midwood |
| 2009 | Blackley | D Townsend |
| 2010 | Sowerby St Peters | G Standeven |
| 2011 | Triangle | C Fletcher |
| 2012 | SBCI | J Sykes |
| 2013 | Jer Lane | M Hustler |

### 1st DIVISION 1st TEAMS

| **Roy Smith Conference** | | | **Terry Wynne Conference** | |
|---|---|---|---|---|
| 2004 | Luddendenfoot | J Hickey | Greetland | G Moody |
| 2005 | Old Crossleyans | J Pearson | King Cross | G Cowgill |
| 2006 | Oxenhope | S Humphreys | Triangle | R D Smith |

## CHANGE IN FORMAT TO A PREMIER DIVISION, FIRST DIVISION AND A SECOND DIVISION
## 1st DIVISION 1st TEAMS

| | | |
|---|---|---|
| 2007 | Old Crossleyans | J Pearson |
| 2008 | Blackley | D Townsend |
| 2009 | Bradshaw | N Jowett |
| 2010 | Copley | M Seraj |
| 2011 | SBCI | J Summerscales |
| 2012 | Mytholmroyd | D Townsend |
| 2013 | Sowerby St Peters | R Brook |

### 2nd DIVISION 1st TEAMS

| | | |
|---|---|---|
| 1954 | Greetland | N E Crossley |
| 1955 | Warley | L Peckover |
| 1956 | Mytholmroyd | K Butterworth |
| 1957 | Bridgeholme | J Horsfall |
| 1958 | Stones | D W Hamer |
| 1959 | Stainland | E Longbottom |
| 1960 | Warley | R Crossley |
| 1961 | Northowram | H Andrew |
| 1962 | Sowerby St Peters | D Habergham |
| 1963 | Triangle | N Ashcroft |
| 1964 | Barkisland | T Schofield |
| 1965 | Crossley's Carpets | T Pollard |

| | | |
|---|---|---|
| 1966 | Copley | T R Thorpe |
| 1967 | Blackley | J Moorhouse |
| 1968 | Copley | B Hulme |
| 1969 | Mytholmroyd Meths | T R Grace |
| 1970 | Northowram | A Butterworth |
| 1971 | Triangle | J Cook |
| 1972 | Warley | R Barker |
| 1973 | Booth | P Metcalfe |
| 1974 | Triangle | J Patrick |
| 1975 | Northowram | A B Kellett |
| 1976 | Crossley's Carpets | T Pollard |
| 1977 | Sowerby St Peters | K Wharvell |
| 1978 | Bradshaw | P Holden |
| 1979 | Stainland | R Malinson |
| 1980 | Greetland | P Nichols |
| 1981 | Mackintosh's | A Ham |
| 1982 | Bradshaw | C Sutcliffe |
| 1983 | Old Town | G Dobby |
| 1984 | Northowram | I Stocks |
| 1985 | Stainland | B Evans |
| 1986 | Luddendenfoot | R D Smith |
| 1987 | S B C I | M Wood |
| 1988 | Outlane | J Smith |
| 1989 | Luddendenfoot | K Weatherill |
| 1990 | Stones | S Milner |
| 1991 | Old Crossleyans | S G Fowler |
| 1992 | Luddendenfoot | S R Smith |
| 1993 | Old Town | N Cowens |
| 1994 | Stones | C Houlker |
| 1995 | Luddendenfoot | S Moore |
| 1996 | Copley | R Bhabra |
| 1997 | Northowram | R Leach |
| 1998 | Luddendenfoot | C Hutchinson |
| 1999 | Sowerby Bridge | T Helliwell |
| 2000 | Sowerby St Peters | M Schofield |
| 2001 | Blackley | J Hey |
| 2002 | Stainland | R Norcliffe |
| 2003 | Thornton | J Ashley |
| 2004 | No Division – Conferences | |
| 2005 | No Division – Conferences | |
| 2006 | No Division – Conferences | |
| 2007 | Jer Lane | J Nixon |
| 2008 | Bridgeholme | K Hudson |
| 2009 | Clayton | P Ayscough |
| 2010 | Wibsey Park Chapel | R Wynn |
| 2011 | Queensbury | J Myers |
| 2012 | Outlane | D Crosland |
| 2013 | Low Moor | N Wood |

# 1st DIVISION 2nd TEAMS

| Year | Team | Player |
|------|------|--------|
| 1914 | Sowerby Bridge | |
| 1915 | Sowerby Bridge | |
| 1916 | League Suspended – World War 1 | |
| 1917 | League Suspended – World War 1 | |
| 1918 | League Suspended – World War 1 | |
| 1919 | League Suspended – No 2nd XI's | |
| 1920 | Mytholmroyd | |
| 1921 | Greetland | |
| 1922 | Greetland | |
| 1923 | Stainland | |
| 1924 | Siddal | |
| 1925 | Siddal | |
| 1926 | Greetland | |
| 1927 | Greetland | |
| 1928 | Clifton Britannia | |
| 1929 | Stainland | |
| 1930 | Greetland | |
| 1931 | Turner & Wainwright's | |
| 1932 | Clifton Britannia | |
| 1933 | Copley | J L Forden |
| 1934 | Mytholmroyd | E Hitchin |
| 1935 | Copley | P E Albon |
| 1936 | Norwood Green | H Kirbyson |
| 1937 | Mytholmroyd | J Dawkins |
| 1938 | Turnwrights & Clifton | G Peacock |
| 1939 | Mytholmroyd | F Walton |
| 1940 | Sowerby St Peters | N Spriggs |
| 1941 | League Suspended – World War 2 | |
| 1942 | League Suspended – World War 2 | |
| 1943 | League Suspended – World War 2 | |
| 1944 | League Suspended – World War 2 | |
| 1945 | League Suspended – World War 2 | |
| 1946 | Mytholmroyd | F Walton |
| 1947 | Mytholmroyd | G A Nicholl |
| 1948 | Mytholmroyd | G Thomas |
| 1949 | Booth | T Patrick |
| 1950 | Mytholmroyd | G Thomas |
| 1951 | Sowerby St Peters | A Gunshon |
| 1962 | Booth | L Patrick |
| 1963 | Sowerby St Peters | G P Dyson |
| 1964 | Sowerby St Peters | G P Dyson |
| 1965 | Booth | K Cockroft |
| 1966 | Triangle | K Wilson |
| 1967 | Booth | K Emmett |
| 1968 | Triangle | K Wilson |
| 1969 | Triangle | K Senior |
| 1970 | Greetland | H A Pidgeon |
| 1971 | Crossley Carpets | S Gledhill |
| 1972 | Triangle | R G Bruce |

| 1973 | Barkisland | D Ward |
| 1974 | Copley | T R Thorpe |
| 1975 | Greetland | L Forester |
| 1976 | Barkisland | S Casaru |
| 1977 | Siddal | D Green |
| 1978 | Copley | H Wood |
| 1979 | Copley | H Wood |
| 1980 | Sowerby St Peters | K Wharvell |
| 1981 | Triangle | K Wilson |
| 1982 | Sowerby St Peters | D Fozzard |
| 1983 | Sowerby St Peters | P Gill |
| 1984 | Barkisland | J Helliwell |
| 1985 | Booth | P Whipp |
| 1986 | Booth | P Whipp |
| 1987 | Barkisland | B Tennyson |
| 1988 | Triangle | J Moore |
| 1989 | Barkisland | P E Rothwell |
| 1990 | Barkisland | R C Attiwell |
| 1991 | Triangle | R J Rodger |
| 1992 | Barkisland | S Casaru |
| 1993 | Booth | G Laycock |
| 1994 | Triangle | J Moore |
| 1995 | Sowerby Bridge | K Hartley |
| 1996 | Triangle | J Moore |
| 1997 | Sowerby Bridge | S Priestley |
| 1998 | Triangle | J Moore |
| 1999 | Triangle | J Moore |
| 2000 | Triangle | J Moore |
| 2001 | Triangle | J Moore |
| 2002 | Triangle | J Moore |
| 2003 | Triangle | J Moore |

## CHANGE IN FORMAT TO A PREMIER DIVISION AND TWO FIRST DIVISION CONFERENCES PREMIERSHIP 2nd TEAMS

| 2004 | Triangle | J Moore |
| 2005 | Sowerby Bridge | A Rushworth |
| 2006 | Mytholmroyd | J Russell |
| 2007 | Sowerby Bridge | A Rushworth |
| 2008 | Triangle | J Moore |
| 2009 | Sowerby Bridge | R Bland |
| 2010 | Sowerby Bridge | R Bland |
| 2011 | Triangle | J Moore |
| 2012 | Warley | J Cooper |
| 2013 | Triangle | J Moore |

# 1st DIVISION 2nd TEAMS

| Roy Smith Conference | | | Terry Wynne Conference | |
|---|---|---|---|---|
| 2004 | Mytholmroyd | J Russell | Thornton | P Butterfield |
| 2005 | Blackley | G Clarke | Bradshaw | B Shierson |
| 2006 | Oxenhope | K Yates | King Cross | J Boddy |

# CHANGE IN FORMAT TO A PREMIER DIVISION, FIRST DIVISION AND A SECOND DIVISION
# 1st DIVISION 2nd TEAMS

| | | |
|---|---|---|
| 2007 | SBCI | M Summerscales |
| 2008 | Blackley | N Crowther |
| 2009 | Booth | N Thomas |
| 2010 | Shelf | N Patefield |
| 2011 | Southowram | D Jowett |
| 2012 | Sowerby St Peters | L Barber |
| 2013 | Jer Lane | M Smith |

# 2nd DIVISION 2nd TEAMS

| | | |
|---|---|---|
| 1956 | Mytholmroyd | R Poxon |
| 1957 | Dean Clough | G Crowther |
| 1958 | Webster's | G Rushby |
| 1959 | Old Town | R Greenwood |
| 1960 | Blackley | G Brook |
| 1961 | Stainland | G Hey |
| 1962 | Dean Clough | K Stringer |
| 1963 | Triangle | E Nicholl |
| 1964 | Copley | R Whiteley |
| 1965 | Sowerby St Peters | E Judson |
| 1966 | Bradshaw | L Dyson |
| 1967 | Stones | H Hallowell |
| 1968 | Stainland | J Lewthwaite |
| 1969 | Stainland | B Norcliffe |
| 1970 | Sowerby St Peters | T Laycock |
| 1971 | Triangle | R G Bruce |
| 1972 | Booth | K Cockroft |
| 1973 | Siddal | D D Nairn |
| 1974 | Sowerby St Peters | M Sheppard |
| 1975 | Mackintosh's | J A Ward |
| 1976 | Mackintosh's | P Steele |
| 1977 | Sowerby St Peters | M Sheppard |
| 1978 | Mytholmroyd | P Williams |
| 1979 | Mytholmroyd Meth's | S Boocock |
| 1980 | Stones | P Collinge |
| 1981 | Mytholmroyd | P Williams |
| 1982 | Old Crossleyans | G Manger |
| 1983 | Mytholmroyd Meth's | D Hunt |

| 1984 | Mytholmroyd | N J Robinson |
| 1985 | Greetland | H Pidgeon |
| 1986 | Blackley | J E Townsend |
| 1987 | Blackley | J E Townsend |
| 1988 | Stones | W Pollard |
| 1989 | Stones | W Pollard |
| 1990 | Stones | W Pollard |
| 1991 | Blackley | D E Peel |
| 1992 | Southowram | P Jowett |
| 1993 | S B C I | S R Hampshire |
| 1994 | Outlane | K Emmett |
| 1995 | Old Town | A Lyons |
| 1996 | Stones | P McDonnell |
| 1997 | S B C I | D Jones |
| 1998 | Copley | S Phipps |
| 1999 | Old Town | A Lyons |
| 2000 | Sowerby St Peters | N Fielden |
| 2001 | Augustinians | S Hazelton |
| 2002 | Blackley | M Burke |
| 2003 | Salendine Nook OB's | C Marriott |
| 2004 | No Division - | Conferences |
| 2005 | No Division - | Conferences |
| 2006 | No Division - | Conferences |
| 2007 | Shelf | P Huddlestone |
| 2008 | Clayton | M Hodgson |
| 2009 | Stones | R Worthington |
| 2010 | Low Moor | D Tempest |
| 2011 | Wibsey Park Chapel | M Overend |
| 2012 | Oxenhope | A Whitehead |
| 2013 | Mytholmroyd | M Bauer |

## LINDLEY MOOR TROPHY

| 1977 | S B C I | A Gawn |
| 1978 | Barkisland | B Tennyson |
| 1979 | Mytholmroyd | D Butterworth |
| 1980 | Warley | A South |
| 1981 | Triangle | T Madden |
| | Old Crossleyans | F Robinson |
| 1982 | Mytholmroyd | M J Astin |
| 1983 | Sowerby St Peters | R Allott |
| 1984 | Mytholmroyd | M J Astin |
| 1985 | Luddendenfoot | S Booth |
| 1986 | Blackley | R S Williams |
| 1987 | Sowerby St Peters | S Crossley |
| 1988 | Sowerby St Peters | S Crossley |
| 1989 | Warley | A Oates |
| 1990 | Blackley | M Eady |
| 1991 | Union Croft | N Robertshaw |
| 1992 | Union Croft | N Robertshaw |
| 1993 | Old Crossleyans | C Daly |

| 1994 | Southowram | V Mylett |
|------|------------|----------|
| 1995 | Mackintosh's | M Reppion |
| 1996 | Outlane | J Smith |
| 1997 | Sowerby Bridge | J Bullick |
| 1998 | Greetland | S Moody |
| 1999 | S B C I | S Scholefield |
| 2000 | S B C I | S Scholefield |
| 2001 | Booth | I Sharkey |
| 2002 | Mytholmroyd Meth's | C Davis |
| 2003 | Northowram Hedge Top | R Leach |
| 2004 | Old Crossleyans | J Pearson |
| 2005 | Oxenhope | D Tetley |
| 2006 | Queensbury | P Sharples |
| 2007 | Low Moor | M Stokes |
| 2008 | Thornton | G Soames |
| 2009 | Wibsey Park Chapel | R Winn |
| 2010 | Shelf | D Maloney |
| 2011 | Booth | Rob Laycock |
| 2012 | Booth | Rob Laycock |
| 2013 | Blackley | T Baxter |

## CLAY TROPHY

| 1987 | Old Town and  S B C I |
|------|-----------------------|
| 1988 | Luddendenfoot |
| 1989 | Barkisland |
| 1990 | S B C I |
| 1991 | S B C I |
| 1992 | Sowerby St Peters |
| 1993 | Warley |
| 1994 | Booth |
| 1995 | Stainland |
| 1996 | Blackley / Old Crossleyans / Southowram (3 way tie) |
| 1997 | Union Croft |
| 1998 | Stainland |
| 1999 | Bradshaw |
| 2000 | Bradshaw |
| 2001 | Sowerby Bridge |
| 2002 | S B C I |
| 2003 | Sowerby Bridge |
| 2004 | King Cross |
| 2005 | Copley |
| 2006 | Stones |
| 2007 | Northowram Hedge Top |
| 2008 | Low Moor |
| 2009 | Northowram Hedge Top |
| 2010 | Triangle |
| 2011 | Blackley |
|      | Bridgeholme |
| 2012 | Mytholmroyd |
| 2013 | Bradshaw |
|      | Thornton |

## TWENTY / 20 CUP COMPETITION WINNERS

| | |
|---|---|
| 2006 | Triangle |
| 2007 | Booth |
| 2008 | Mytholmroyd |
| 2009 | Jer Lane |
| 2010 | Sowerby St Peters |
| 2011 | Jer Lane |
| 2012 | Southowram |
| 2013 | Thornton |

## SPORTSMAN OF THE YEAR TROPHY
## AN INDIVIDUAL AWARD - PRESENTED BY THE
## HALIFAX CRICKET LEAGUE UMPIRES ASSOCIATION

| | |
|---|---|
| 1978 | J Barron |
| 1979 | R Walters |
| 1980 | T Firth |
| 1981 | A Brook |
| 1982 | A Gawn |
| 1983 | L Dyson |
| 1984 | F Hemmingway |
| 1985 | P Metcalfe |
| 1986 | J Mitchell |
| 1987 | G Newsome |
| 1988 | A P Houlker |
| 1989 | C A Hagues |
| 1990 | T Pollard |
| 1991 | J Parker |
| 1992 | P Holden |
| 1993 | P Marsh |
| 1994 | T Laycock |
| 1995 | R Severn |
| 1996 | R D Rodger |
| 1997 | A Schofield |
| 1998 | C Sutcliffe |
| 1999 | M Ellis |
| 2000 | M Wood |
| 2001 | J Hoyle |
| 2002 | M Thomas |
| 2003 | M Pettengell |
| 2004 | J Cliff |
| 2005 | K Hudson |
| 2006 | P Reynolds |
| 2007 | R S Williams |
| 2008 | N Myers |
| 2009 | H Cooper |
| 2010 | D Normanton |
| 2011 | N Thomas |
| 2012 | N Crosland |
| 2013 | C Charles |

## ROY SMITH SPORTSMANSHIP TROPHY
## A CLUB AWARD - MARKED BY THE
## HALIFAX CRICKET LEAGUE UMPIRES ASSOCIATION

| | |
|---|---|
| 1997 | Stones |
| 1998 | Stones |
| 1999 | Stones |
| 2000 | Copley |
| 2001 | Booth |
| 2002 | Stones |
| 2003 | Booth |
| 2004 | Luddendenfoot |
| 2005 | Northowram Hedge Top |
| 2006 | Bradshaw |
| 2007 | Northowram Hedge Top |
| 2008 | Outlane |
| 2009 | Stainland |
| 2010 | Luddendenfoot |
| 2011 | Copley |
| 2012 | Wibsey Park Chapel |
| 2013 | Greetland |

## UNIVERSITY OF HUDDERSFIELD
## HISTORY & HERITAGE AWARD

| | |
|---|---|
| 2006 | Queensbury |
| 2007 | Bradshaw |
| 2008 | Augustinians |
| 2009 | Stones and Warley |
| 2010 | Southowram |
| 2011 | Blackley |
| 2012 | Triangle |
| 2013 | Halifax Cricket League |

| Member Clubs 2014 | Ground Altitude (In Metres) |
|---|---|
| **1.** Blackley CC | **207** |
| **2.** Booth CC | **182** |
| **3.** Bradshaw CC | **280** |
| **4.** Bridgeholme CC | **141** |
| **5.** Clayton CC | **225** |
| **6.** Copley CC | **66** |
| **7.** Cullingworth CC | **188** |
| **8.** Denholme Clough CC | **311** |
| **9.** Greetland CC | **68** |
| **10.** Jer Lane CC | **280** |
| **11.** Low Moor Holy Trinity CC | **164** |
| **12.** Luddendenfoot CC | **205** |
| **13.** Mytholmroyd CC | **89** |
| **14.** Northowram Hedge Top CC | **219** |
| **15.** Old Crossleyans CC | **156** |
| **16.** Old Town CC | **265** |
| **17.** Outlane CC | **260** |
| **18.** Oxenhope CC | **219** |
| **19.** Queensbury CC | **363** |
| **20.** Shelf CC | **258** |
| **21.** Southowram CC | **220** |
| **22.** Sowerby Bridge CC | **77** |
| **23.** SBCI CC | **194** |
| **24.** Sowerby St. Peter's CC | **190** |
| **25.** Stainland CC | **208** |
| **26.** Stones CC | **266** |
| **27.** Thornton CC | **256** |
| **28.** Triangle CC | **99** |
| **29.** Warley CC | **226** |
| **30.** Wibsey Park Chapel CC | **165** |

# CONCLUSION

The publication of this book would not have been possible without the immense support of clubs, club members, patrons and advertisers.

This is a tribute to all those who have worked for and supported our League down the first 100 years.

This book was launched at the Shay Stadium, Halifax on Friday 9th May 2014 at the Centenary Dinner Celebration when the guest speaker was Matthew James Hoggard MBE, former England, Yorkshire and Leicestershire cricketer.

Matthew James Hoggard OBE

I hope that anyone who has been involved with local cricket will find that in reading this book it has brought back memories of how their own lives have been influenced by a club in which they are involved or reminds them of visits made to local cricket grounds in their lifetime.

Yours in Cricket - David Normanton
President Halifax Cricket League